AMERICAN
MARKETING
ASSOCIATION

Higher Profits through Customer Lock-in: A Roadmap

Joachim Büschken

THOMSON

SOUTH-WESTERN

Australia · Canada · Mexico · Singapore · Spain · United Kingdom · United States

THOMSON™

Higher Profits Through Customer Lock-In: A Roadmap
Joachim Büschken

COPYRIGHT © 2004 by TEXERE, an imprint of Thomson Business and Professional Publishing, a part of the Thomson Corporation. Thomson, the Star logo, TEXERE, and Thomson Business and Professional Publishing are trademarks used herein under license.

ISBN: 0-324-20265-2
Printed and bound in the United States of America by Phoenix Color
1 2 3 4 5 6 7 8 9 07 06 05 04

For more information, contact Texere at Thomson Learning, 5191 Natorp Boulevard, Mason, OH 45040. You can also visit our website at www.thomson.com/learning/texere

Composed by: Navta Associates, Inc.

A CIP catalogue record for this book is available from the Library of Congress.
Library of Congress Control Number: 2004108424

TABLE OF CONTENTS

ACKNOWLEDGEMENTS

Sometimes you don't know what you're getting into. This is certainly true with this book. About two years ago, Michael Czinkota, a marketing professor at Georgetown University and a dear colleague, approached me with the idea of writing a book for the U.S. market. He knew what I was doing here in Germany and he felt that I should go global. After all, he thinks that global marketing "is imperative." And isn't that true? So in a way Michael is responsible for me starting this project and, without this initial impetus, you wouldn't be holding it in your hands. Thank you, Michael.

Michael also put me in touch with Steve Momper, head of professional publishing at Thomson. Steve quickly grasped the idea behind this book and provided invaluable support throughout the process. I extend my deepest gratitude to Steve for his relentless efforts to improve the quality of the manuscript. He read various drafts in depth and provided invaluable suggestions at every stage. In doing so, he helped me to improve the book tremendously. What more can you ask for in an editor?

My dear friend and colleague, Professor Christoph Burmann of University of Bremen in Germany, provided some painful commentary on an early manuscript and a heartfelt "thank you" is therefore in order—not for the pain but for what came out of it. Felicitas Nogly, a very capable graduate student at Catholic University of Eichstätt-Ingolstadt (and now a Ph.D. student), has provided support in case research. It is with great pleasure that I acknowledge her important assistance in this project.

Catholic University endured my extended leave of absence, during which I was able to concentrate on writing this book. My thanks go to Claudia Kreye, Stephan Erlenkämper, Robert Heim, and Rainer Schlamp in the Marketing Department for shouldering my duties.

The most important contribution to this book was provided by a man I have never met—to my deepest regret. In 1989 I received a full one-year Fulbright scholarship which enabled me to study in the MBA program of Texas A&M University. The fact that this wonderful exchange program exists is largely owed to the late Senator William J. Fulbright whose far-reaching vision has led to one of the most successful educational exchange programs in the world. Without this program, I would never have been able to study in the United States, really learn the language and—ultimately—write this book. In times like these, visionary leaders like Senator Fulbright are very much missed.

To Daniela, Rachel, and Lea
and, of course,
Moritz, the Bear

PREFACE

Higher Profits through Customer Lock-in:
A Roadmap

This book is based on a rather simple notion. Customers with switching costs are more loyal and present higher profit potential than those who can switch brands or suppliers any time. Switching costs account for a substantial part of the profits in industries such as banking and inkjet printers. They depict any kind of financial or emotional burden for customers that prevent them from switching from one brand or supplier to another. Switching costs result in a "lock-in" effect: customers can't easily switch on a whim. Customer lock-in can produce significantly higher profits. Therefore, strategy should be targeted at creating switching costs for customers.

In the following chapters of this book, all relevant elements of a profit-enhancing strategy based on switching costs are discussed. The most important elements of this discussion are:

- Switching costs are a significant profit-driver in many industries. They provide monopolistic power—the ultimate goal in marketing. In simpler terms: They allow charging higher prices. Higher prices lead to higher profits. For a detailed discussion, see chapters 1 and 2.
- It is vital to understand the economics of markets with switching costs. Chapters 4 and 5 are dedicated to this topic. There is no automatism between switching costs and higher profits. Managers need to know which kind of lock-in-based price discrimination works and which doesn't. The underlying drivers of market structure and industry rivalry must be carefully analyzed. Among the many factors important in industry analysis, complements play a crucial role. They are the cornerstone of higher profits through customer lock-in.
- Switching costs will change the way your customers choose among alternative brands and suppliers. It is vital to understand the changes in buying behavior and their implications for your strategy. Also, the way you need to segment your market is affected. Different market segments pose very different marketing challenges—up to the point where it is impossible to recruit new customers and enhance the value of the customer base at the same time. For that discussion, see chapters 6 and 7.
- When developing the strategy, you need to be aware of market segments ("entrenched users," "new buyers") interacting

with each other (see chapter 13). This requires a clear understanding of how to target market segments.

- There are various instruments used to create customer lock-in. They all raise distinctive management issues. In particular, bonus and discount programs can severely backfire. Learn from the leaders and avoid the pitfalls. Both are discussed in great detail in chapters 7–12.

- Implementing the strategy leads to new challenges in marketing. Don't think that creating switching costs is easy to do. What you need is an integrated and adapted marketing system to raise the profit potential. See chapters 13–17.

- You can't manage what you can't measure. Chapter 18 addresses the issue of how to measure the impact of lock-in on customer equity. What's important here? Don't just count customers or their purchases—measure their degree of lock-in. This is the key driver of future revenues. As a manager, you should be concerned more with the future than the past.

- Implementation of the lock-in strategy requires adaptation of your organization in terms of structure and culture. Be prepared to address these issues (chapter 19).

This book provides the first comprehensive discussion of strategy based on customer switching costs. It's worth it to take a look. For further information go to www.customerlockin.com.

Why Is Customer Lock-in Important?

Customer lock-in is important because it increases profits. Compared to the popular customer satisfaction doctrine, it is a very different approach to thinking about the supplier–customer relationship. For most companies, programs to increase customer satisfaction have been costly, but not profitable. In many cases, higher customer satisfaction does not lead to higher customer loyalty.

Customer lock-in occurs when customers have significant switching costs. Switching costs place a financial and/or emotional burden on the customer who intends to switch brands or suppliers. Not surprisingly, customer loyalty in industries with significant switching costs is much higher. In extreme cases, customers become the economic hostage of original brand selection.

The following chapters focus on the origin of switching costs and their impact on profits. Empirical analysis shows that switching costs drive retention rates up and facilitate profitable price discrimination. For many companies, customer satisfaction can't deliver the same results.

Getting Out of the Customer Satisfaction Trap

THE CUSTOMER SATISFACTION TRAP

Ever since the rise of Japanese car makers and manufacturers of electronic equipment, the importance of quality and customer satisfaction has been stressed. Managers all over the world are pursuing programs to measure and enhance customer satisfaction with near-religious furor to improve relationships to customers, and to increase customer loyalty and, ultimately, the profitability of their business.

This trend has been fuelled by extensive academic research on the relationship between customer satisfaction and profits. There are now so many studies supporting this view, it's hard to keep track. Again and again, we hear:

- Customer Satisfaction (CS) drives loyalty, which, in turn, drives profits. This is due to higher costs of customer acquisition versus lower costs of customer retention.
- There is a strong relationship between customer satisfaction and a company's market capitalization. Some studies claim that a 1% increase in CS produces a 3% increase in market capitalization.

Why, then, do even highly satisfied consumers defect? Why is CS a bad predictor of a buyer's intention to allocate business to a certain supplier? Why do so many customer-relationship management (CRM) projects fail? Industry observers report CRM project failure rates of 60–70% indicating that CRM often fails to improve the profitability of the firm.

All these facts are troubling. One popular explanation is that implementing effective CRM is difficult and requires more changes to the organization than expected. Often, costs exceed projections. Therefore, industry experts urge you not to lose faith in the importance of customer satisfaction.

I suggest you should place a lower importance on customer satisfaction. Customer satisfaction is a trap. If your experience is that CS improvement has not brought the results you need, stop digging. The hole you're in is only getting deeper. There is sound empirical evidence strongly suggesting that, in general, customer satisfaction is *not* a significant customer loyalty or profit driver. Or, more specifically, it is only under specific circumstances:

- In *competitive markets* with options to choose from and quality-sensitive customers who pay (enough) for additional quality. Without choice, as in a monopoly, CS plays no role. The customer's only alternative is *not* to buy.
- Where potential for customer satisfaction improvement exists and instruments for CS improvement can, for some time, be *protected* against competitive duplication.
- That *customer switching costs* play no role in the purchasing process.

The automobile industry fits that description. Many car manufacturers and brands compete on high quality levels constituting sufficient choice for customers in various market segments. Customers are quality-sensitive. This means that higher perceived quality can increase willingness to pay. With many options available, lack of customer satisfaction and the threat to switch brands is a significant incentive for car manufacturers to deliver quality.

In this industry, important product features improving customer satisfaction can be protected against imitation for some time. Think of Chrysler's invention of the U.S. minivan segment (as with Renault in Europe). It took Ford (VW in Europe) years to react and offer competitive models similar in size and seating arrangement. Toyota's lean production process combining highly efficient production (read: cost advantage) with high product quality (read: price advantage) is another. Even after an MIT study "uncovered" the relevance of lean production, it took competitors years to successfully implement this system. Only product attributes and proprietary processes can create a sustainable customer satisfaction advantage.

If product elements or service processes relevant to customer satisfaction can easily be copied by competitors, their long-term impact on a competitive customer satisfaction *advantage* is zero. They offer no potential for a *sustainable* competitive advantage based on customer satisfaction. This can be observed in the hotel industry in which many service elements (e.g. high-speed checkout, club membership privileges) are ubiquitous or subject to fast imitation. Fast imitation leads to ever-increasing customer quality expectations. This is a cost-intensive marketing strategy without a real potential for sustainable profitability.

For CS to "work," the absence of customer-switching costs is very important. Switching costs prevent unsatisfied customers from immediately changing to a different supplier, even if that offer is better. Switching costs are any kind of barrier for customers to freely change brands or suppliers. If switching costs exist, a company's strategies to improve CS cannot be directly translated into market share. Customers may observe the quality improvement, but they are unable to act accordingly. A relative loss in CS will not lead to customers defecting. An improvement in quality will not lead to brand change.

AN ALTERNATIVE STRATEGY: CUSTOMER LOCK-IN THROUGH SWITCHING COSTS

An alternative strategy is to create customer switching costs. Switching costs are any type of financial or emotional barrier that prevents customers from switching between brands or suppliers. In the event of such switching costs, the logical chain between customer satisfaction and loyalty breaks down.

Consider the case of HP's (Hewlett-Packard's) Imaging and Printing Division:

HP makes its money largely with its imaging and printing (IP) division. To be specific, this profit mainly comes from the sales of printing supplies. For 2002, industry experts estimated that 30–35% of HP's total profit came from the sales of printer cartridges, about half of the IP division's profit.

Printing and imaging has always been the backbone of HP's business. With sales of $14.7 bn in fiscal year 2002, this segment has earned $2.3 bn, more than HP's total operating profit. With printer prices going down and HP printer cartridge prices increasing contrary to industry trends, HP's profit at the moment largely comes from individuals and small businesses that have to purchase expensive supplies for their HP printers.

Walter Hewlett has sharply criticized the merger with Compaq, because it "would significantly dilute HP's stockholder interest in the profitable imaging and printing business". Industry experts and analysts hotly debate whether HP should hold on to businesses not directly related to printing and imaging. It is quite unclear whether the merger with Compaq will help HP to sustain the profitability of its printing business.

Why is HP able to sustain above-normal profits in its printing division?

The answer lies in the prices of printer cartridges. It is no industry secret that printers are often sold at, or even below, cost. The cheapest HP color inkjet printers are currently offered at $50–100, a low-end laser printer at around $250. In contrast, cartridges are expensive. A set of original HP inkjet cartridges costs $60–80—about as much as a black-and-white laser printer cartridge. Production costs for an inkjet cartridge are $4–5. Buyers typically use their printer for 3–4 years, purchasing several sets of cartridges during that time. What makes HP's printing and imaging division so profitable is the HP printer owner's acceptance of huge markups for printing supplies to keep their inkjet printers "up and running."

Why should customers pay high prices for their printer's consumables? Because they perceive significant switching costs. HP (among others) has been very successful in implementing switching costs. Switching from "original" HP cartridges to non-brand cartridges can be costly.

Customers first have to spend search costs to find supplies that work just as well as the HP-brand products. Besides ink, the cartridges in some inkjet printers contain part of the printing technology that can not legally be copied. Thus, pure imitation of HP printer cartridges for inkjets is protected by patent law. Alternatively, non-brand suppliers have specialized in refilling original cartridges or providing refill sets for users. Refilled cartridges ("remanufactured") typically cost half the price of new cartridges. Refill kits are even cheaper.

HP warns customers against the use of such supplies. It claims that refills cannot maintain a high level of printing quality and may even damage printer hardware. HP writes on its homepage:

> "HP does not recommend using refilled print cartridges in HP Inkjet printers. Damage resulting from the modification of or refilling of HP Inkjet cartridges is specifically excluded from coverage in HP printer warranties." It states further: "Damage resulting from the modification or refilling of HP cartridges is specifically excluded from coverage in HP printer warranties."[1]

Similar claims are made by Epson. Until now HP and others have been successful at fending off suppliers of remanufactured cartridges and refill sets such as TonerPlus or Refillink.Com who are estimated to

---

1 Source: http://www.hp.com/cpo-support/printers/support_doc/ bpa00113.html

have a combined 11% market share of the $27 bn U.S. cartridge market. Considering the price differential of 100%, this is very little. It is obvious that most customers are highly reluctant to switch to "unauthorized" suppliers—mostly explained by the perceived risk of inferior printing quality and possible loss of warranty. In other words, customers perceive risk-induced switching costs. These switching costs enable HP and others to charge high prices for cartridges.

This example demonstrates the tremendous power of customer lock-in, beginning when HP, Epson and Lexmark sell high-quality inkjet printers to customers at cost. The profit then comes from selling proprietary supplies to users who are reluctant to switch to non-brand sources. The fact that original-brand cartridges still own 90% of the U.S. market at prices twice as high as knockoffs tells us something about the power of switching costs. It helps that distributors have little interest in aggressively promoting cheaper versions from rivals that diminish their own profits.

Attracted by the profits that can be achieved by selling printer supplies, Dell has announced that it will enter the printer market in cooperation with Lexmark. It will be interesting to see whether HP can sustain its margin on printer supplies following this market entry. Another threat to HP may come from the EU commission's investigation as to whether manufacturers use illegal tactics to force consumers to buy brand cartridges instead of cheaper versions made by rivals.

The HP printer case presents an important issue: If customers incur costs to switch to another brand, then competition follows different rules. Customers become inert. They cannot freely choose between brands after they have committed to a certain technology. As a result, the influence of customer satisfaction on customer loyalty is diminished.

In effect, HP—and all companies creating lock-in—face two types of customers: Those who own an HP printer and those who do not. Brand owners are locked in for as long as they wish to use their printer. Overwhelmingly, they choose to buy supplies from the brand maker. This is largely independent from customer satisfaction. Customers looking to purchase a new printer may consider the cost of after-sales supplies, but they are faced with similar consequences no matter which printer brand they choose.

Interestingly, over time most customers move from brand to brand with the end of the use of a certain printer and the decision to replace it with a new one. In part 3, we will look more closely at market segmentation driven by switching costs.

WHAT ARE SWITCHING COSTS?

Switching costs are any costs associated with changing from one brand or supplier to another. Switching costs include all costs of terminating the relationship to a brand or supplier and setting up a new one until it provides the same benefits. We all experience switching costs under many circumstances. Switching costs originate from technology (as with printer cartridges) or pricing, as in the case of accumulated frequent flyer miles. In each case, they present a barrier to switch between brands. In effect, switching costs increase customer loyalty.

Mortgages are an excellent example to demonstrate the power of switching costs. Let's say that you have taken out a mortgage to finance your home. The U.K. consumer choice service WHICH? gives four reasons to consider switching a mortgage or the lender (www.switchwithwhich.co.uk):

- to benefit from a lower interest rate
- to switch from a variable interest rate to a fixed or capped rate if you think rates are going to rise
- to release equity in your property
- to switch to a more flexible mortgage if you want to be able to alter the pattern of your payments

Switching mortgages—as you probably know—can be very costly, consisting of several elements. There is often an early repayment charge. This is a penalty the lender charges when a loan is partially or fully repaid early. Depending on the kind of arrangement (for example, with fixed or capped rates), this can be a several thousand dollar penalty. Additional costs may be incurred for credit searches, property appraisals and so on. Also, the new lender might charge some sort of sealing or arrangement fee. It is advisable to switch your mortgage if total switching costs are less than the savings realized from reduced interest rates with the new mortgage over the same period of time.

What does that mean? You will only switch a mortgage if the interest rate differential between the current and new mortgage is large enough to at least cover your switching costs. This means that the current lender can charge a premium over competitive offers without having his customers switch. The size of this premium depends on the switching costs: The higher they are, the higher is that premium. In simple words, this is the power of customer lock-in.

ADDING SHAREHOLDER VALUE THROUGH CUSTOMER LOCK-IN

Customer lock-in adds substantial value to company strategy; therefore, every company should be concerned with the degree their customers are locked in to their brands. The three principal shareholder value drivers are:

1. The ability to enhance future cash flows through extending the market (acquiring new customers) or to cross-sell to existing customers.
2. The ability to accelerate cash-flows. This can be achieved by speeding up product development and market penetration.
3. The ability to reduce the volatility of cash-flows. This increases the retention rate of your customer base and achieves higher stability of the revenue stream.

Customer lock-in increases the extractable value from a customer base in more than one way. It enhances the ability to cross- and up-sell once customers are locked in to a brand or solution. Switching costs prevent customers from switching brands freely. Hilton, for example, extracts 50% of its profits from only 3% of its guests. These guests are Gold and Silver members of Hilton's loyalty reward program who have strong incentives to stay brand-loyal in order to access rewards. In general, they stay longer, book more expensive rooms (up-selling), and buy more service while there (cross-selling). Switching costs reduce the volatility of cash-flows. Many Microsoft users are heavily locked into the idiosyncrasies of Office technology and their brand-loyalty is extremely high, resulting in a high probability of nearly all current users adopting new releases of Office Suite.

BMW had a very different experience with the introduction of its new 7-series in Germany. The design of this car is so unusual that many owners of old 7 models decided to switch to other—and less profitable—BMW models or even to switch the brand. This happens when there are little or no switching costs.

Customer lock-in adds value because it changes the focus of a company's strategy dramatically. Traditionally, the key elements of marketing strategy (segmentation, selection of target markets, positioning) center on customer preference. A preference indicates what option the customer likes more in comparison to another option and is expressed in terms such as: "I like Coke Light more than Diet Pepsi." Customer preference is often fuzzy, changes rapidly, and is always subject to new products from competitors. How does a company deal with variety-seeking customers who perceive brand change itself as beneficial? In other words, preference is a somewhat precarious concept to build a strategy on.

Customer-switching costs present an alternative concept that shields companies from abrupt customer preference changes and competitive influences. Brand preference is a good customer trait, but loyalty based on switching costs is much better.

WHAT THIS BOOK IS ABOUT AND HOW IT CAN HELP YOU

The basic idea behind this book is that customer lock-in breaks the link between customer satisfaction, loyalty, and, ultimately, profits. When switching costs are relevant, lock-in becomes a more important driver of a company's performance than customer satisfaction. With customer lock-in, customers *must* be loyal to a certain company. Customer lock-in is a golden handcuff: For a certain period of time, customers cannot escape.

The following issues are important.

1. What is the impact of switching costs on industry? What can we learn from switching-cost rich industries? What can we learn from economic theory? These are the most important questions to be discussed in the remaining sections of part 1.
2. Are markets with switching costs different? In what way? These questions lie at the heart of part 2.
3. How can companies create switching costs? How can these instruments be managed? What are the pitfalls companies should avoid? Part 3 covers these issues.
4. What problems arise with the mastering of lock-in? What are the consequences for a company's segmentation strategy? How is the customer potential analyzed for a switching-cost driven strategy? How do customers migrate from zero to high switching costs? What are the implications of that strategy for your organization? These strategic implications of switching costs are discussed in part 4.

This book will provide a sound framework to direct a strategic approach to customer lock-in. Customer lock-in is a very different approach than customer satisfaction and it requires substantial changes to strategy development and execution. We will go through that process step-by-step. The ultimate goal is, of course, to improve profits. This is not an easy task. Don't fall into a new trap by thinking that once customers have switching costs they can be milked. No path to higher profits is that simple. Customer lock-in requires a thoughtful, well-devised strategy that navigates companies around the cliffs and shallow waters of competition. Enjoy the journey!

2

Customer Lock-in in Action

IMPACT OF SWITCHING COSTS: A LOOK AT VARIOUS INDUSTRIES

Switching costs are very powerful industry drivers, strongly impacting the behavior of all players. Although empirical research on the consequences of switching costs is relatively scarce, we have learned some important lessons from that research. It highlights the relevance of customer switching costs in various industries.

Banking

Switching costs are highly relevant to the banking industry. It can be very costly to transfer debt between financial institutions. Do you think a loan is a commodity? Be assured, *before* it is taken out. After taking out a loan, debt is very heterogeneous. It cannot be transferred easily and without costs between financial institutions. Estimating the switching costs of debt is not an easy undertaking. Service providers such as www.themovechannel.com and www. mortgageexposed.com offer remortgage cost calculators that offer interesting insights into the switching costs for mortgages.

In a study of the U.S. banking structure from 1980–1998, the Federal Reserve Board concluded that switching costs "are an increasingly important characteristic of retail banking." This is a modest way of saying that switching costs reduce competition on the retail level, provide market power, and create higher interest rates for loans, mortgages, and credit card balances.

An empirical study commissioned by the Central Bank of Norway shows that switching costs account for about one-third of loan interest rates in Norway. In other words: in an environment without switching costs, loan interest rates would be 33% lower.[1] The study also found that larger

1 Source: Study by M. Kim, D. Klinger and B. Vale (2003).

customers such as companies have lower switching costs. Companies can more easily transfer debt and receive financial services elsewhere than can consumers. Not surprisingly, companies usually pay lower interest rates than consumers.

This means there is a direct relationship between switching costs and consumer prices in the banking industry. Higher switching costs lead to higher prices and, consequently, to higher profits.

Mobile Phone Services

The mobile phone service industry is highly competitive. With 122 million subscribers in America, 287 million in Western Europe and 316 million in Asia, the mobile phone industry is approaching saturation. Adoption rates of 80% in Hong Kong and the United Kingdom are typical signs of mature industries. This industry typically offers subsidized hardware (the mobile phone) in exchange for a commitment to one- or two-year service contracts. For that time, the customer is economically locked-in. The service contract cannot be terminated without payment of the monthly subscription fee for the remainder of the contract length. Other switching costs include the possible loss of the phone number and search costs when shopping for a better deal. Thus, virtually no customer terminates the service contract prematurely. Most customers wait until the contract is about to expire and then shop around. In the past, customers have been reluctant to change carriers because of the non-portability of cell phone numbers between providers.

Earl Sasser and Thomas Jones from Harvard Business School have coined this type of customer the "hostage," referring to a moderately satisfied or even unsatisfied customer who remains loyal due to switching costs embedded in the contract. If switching costs are high, the customer will not defect.

In the mobile phone industry, switching costs were found to moderate the satisfaction-loyalty link. The strength of this link depends on the amount of switching costs involved in a supplier-customer relationship. Switching costs between mobile phone service providers are very high as long as the standard contract has not expired. The higher the switching costs are, the more loyal customers are. Under extreme circumstances (very high switching costs prohibiting any exit) this is a "forced loyalty," against the customer's preferences.

Bear in mind that empirical research on the customer satisfaction-loyalty link also depends on how loyalty is measured. Two

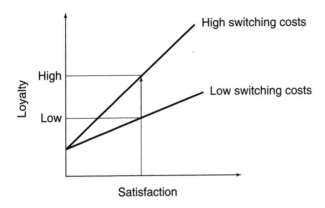

Figure 2-1: Switching Costs Moderating the Satisfaction-Loyalty Link
(Source: J. Lee, J. Lee, and L. Feick, 2001)

approaches are possible—to measure loyalty on the basis of actual behavior, which lies in the past, or to measure repurchase intention, which is an attitudinal measure. In the presence of switching costs, unsatisfied customers may have a very low repurchase intention but may be locked-in for a considerable period of time. Behavior may then be very different than behavior based on preference or attitude.

Loyalty and share of wallet are not the same thing. A customer who re-buys from a certain vendor is "loyal." This says nothing about the degree to which related purchases are concentrated, such as add-on capacity or complementary items to this vendor. Those are share of wallet. Economically, we are more interested in share of wallet rather than loyalty.

Information Technology

One of the most prominent examples of the influence of switching costs on purchase behavior can be found in the information technology industry. Buying IT hardware or software often results in making vendor-specific investments into specific human resources (know-how) to use it properly. Many people have invested to some degree into Microsoft-specific know-how that is necessary to use Microsoft software effectively. This investment prevents most people from changing to alternative suppliers such as open source Linux or Star Office from Sun.

The same is true for IT hardware. In the U.S. workstation market, switching costs due to vendor-specific investments were found to decrease the number of suppliers considered in the purchase process, resulting in a strong tendency to stick to "proven suppliers."[2] This tendency is even stronger if buyers are concerned with the compatibility of new technology, and if the pace of technology development is high. Then, switching may be very risky.

Toll-free Services

The toll-free or so-called "800-service" is an essential marketing instrument and service product especially for consumer goods makers. It offers a cost-effective and direct communication tool with consumers that otherwise would have little or no personal contact with a consumer goods manufacturer.

Prior to May 1993, U.S. toll-free service customers could not change their toll-free service provider without being assigned a new toll-free number. Thus, changing the service provider imposed significant switching costs to companies with a well established 800 number. The new number would have to be communicated to consumers on product labels, in advertisements, changed on business cards and so on.

After May 1993, technological advances made it possible to change service providers without changing the 800 number ("portability"), which dramatically reduced switching costs. An empirical study, by Brian Viard of Stanford, shows that portability of the 800 number induced AT&T to reduce the contribution margin (price minus marginal costs divided by price) by an average of 14% across all contracts. In an industry with nearly homogenous products, a sustainable 14% markup is substantial. This confirms that prices in competitive markets are directly related to switching costs because they provide market power.

Prior to May 1993, 800-service providers charged the same price to new and old customers. In other words, price discrimination between new and old (for example, locked-in) customers was forbidden. AT&T as well as other service providers such as Sprint and MCI had to decide whether to price high and milk its existing customer base, or to attract new customers in a rapidly-growing market into its customer base with low prices. Thus, AT&T's price reduction indicates that milking the customer base had a higher priority than attracting new customers. If prices would not have changed, this would have indicated that, prior to May 1993, attraction of new customers was more important than exploiting the existing customer base.

Recently, federal telecommunication regulation made it possible for cell phone users to keep their number when switching

---

2 Source: Study by J. B. Heide and A. Weiss (1995).

between providers. According to a recent NYT article, this has led to a sharp increase in switching activity.[3] Portability of cell phone numbers has reduced switching costs significantly. A drastic impact on providers' ability to charge high prices for their services will surely follow.

Gasoline

It is hard to imagine a market with less product differentiation than gasoline. Gasoline is sold to drivers from gas stations carrying different brands, but little do most people care what company actually produces the gas we are using. However, gasoline is differentiated by the location of gas stations, which may be nearer to some customers and further away for others. The cost of driving to a gas station (so called "search costs") has an impact on consumer behavior.

There are so many gas stations that the search cost for obtaining gas seems to be a minor problem. Empirical research shows, however, that location was responsible for a persistent price differentiation between leaded and unleaded gasoline in the United States in the 1980s. During this time, many gas stations terminated the sale of leaded gas which was unsuitable for cars with modern exhaust control systems. This contributed to higher average costs that customers incurred in order to obtain leaded gas— they simply had to drive longer to buy gas. Increased switching costs between alternative sources of supply followed. Accordingly, the few gas stations selling leaded gas could obtain a significant markup over the price of unleaded gas that was unrelated to production and selling costs.

Summary

What do these industries teach us about the impact of switching costs? Here are the most important lessons.

- Switching costs are relevant in many industries. The cases discussed here range from banking to IT hardware. They are relevant in business-to-consumer (B2C) as well as in business-to-business (B2B) settings. Thus, the impact of switching costs is not limited to specific industries. They are capable of differentiating commodities such as gasoline.

---

3 Source: M. Richtel: The Lines are Busy as Cellphone Clients Switch, New York Times, 25.11.2003.

- Switching costs result from vendor-specific investments made by the customer. Once a person has chosen a toll-free or mobile phone service provider, switching becomes costly. Companies invest in informing their target market about the company's toll-free or mobile phone number. If the number is not portable, this investment is lost. Portability for toll-free phone numbers has existed in the United States since 1993 and has driven prices down. In the German mobile phone market, portability has existed since late 2002. The impact on prices as a result of reduced switching costs remains to be seen. But, surely, price competition will increase as a result of reduced switching costs.
- Switching costs provide market power to companies with locked-in customers. This market power comes from hetero-geneity of products or services *after* the first purchase has been made. Due to switching costs, even a commodity like money becomes heterogeneous when a loan is to be trans-ferred between financial institutions.
- Market power translates into pricing power. This means a company with an existing customer base can choose between raising prices to exploit the lock-in effect or lowering prices to attract new customers into its customer base. The AT&T case shows that raising prices to favor existing customers can be advantageous, even in rapidly growing industries.
- Switching costs soften the customer satisfaction/loyalty rela-tionship. This link is often assumed to be a general causal (and positive) relationship, which is not true. In the case of significant switching costs, even highly unsatisfied customers are loyal.

Clearly, companies that induce customers to invest into their brands can create a sustainable competitive advantage. Brand-specific investment results in lock-in that keeps customers loyal. This loyalty translates into market and pricing power. Empirical research on the impact of switching costs is consistent in observ-ing that lock-in leads to higher prices. The relationship between prices and profits is clear.

TYPES OF SWITCHING COSTS

Transactional Switching Costs

When a person changes his bank account, he needs to close the old account and open a new account with another bank. The time and effort spent on that transaction are **transactional switching costs.** Included are search costs when shopping for a better deal. Also, driving (further) to a different gas station that sells cheaper gas involves (higher) transactional switching costs.

Consumers incur transactional switching costs every time they visit a bookstore or any other kind of retail establishment. Once there, it is costly to find a different store. This is why bookstores such as Barnes & Noble discount books in high demand.

> At a first glance, this practice is quite puzzling. Why should a bookstore discount bestsellers when they are in high demand? Shouldn't products in high demand be sold at high prices? For Borders or Barnes & Noble it is typical to offer discounts of 30% or more on current bestsellers. Discounts on certain items are supposed to attract buyers into the store who will incur search costs for full-price items that they don't plan to buy there.

> Let's say a person wants to buy the newest Harry Potter book. It is on sale at Barnes & Noble at a 40% discount. The consumer drives to the mall and goes to the B&N store to find a copy. At that point, the shopper has transactional switching costs for any other books that are found while browsing. These are costs incurred for finding another bookstore in which to purchase the other items. Another bookstore might be next door, which means transactional switching costs are small. Or another store might be miles away, meaning that the transactional switching costs are high. Consequently, B&N can charge higher prices for items that are bundled "on the spot" with bestsellers because of such switching costs.

Bestsellers are loss-leaders. Bookstores have little interest in extracting buyers' willingness to pay for bestsellers. At Barnes & Noble, bestsellers account for less than 3% of sales. It is much more profitable to use bestsellers (or comparable items) as creators of transactional switching costs.[4] This strategy pays if buyers routinely bundle bestsellers with additional, regularly priced items.

---

4 Transactional switching costs are lower with on-line retailers. This is why on-line bookstores offer lower discounts on bestsellers. See: T.S. Lee and I. Png: Buyer Switching Costs: On-Line vis-à-vis Conventional Retailing, Working Paper, School of Computing, National University of Singapore, July 2002, available at: http://www.comp.nus.edu.sg/~tlee/books_jie2.pdf

Transactional switching costs are incurred every time suppliers are switched. Sometimes companies reduce the cost of switching to them, thereby creating *asymmetric switching costs.* Your new bank may offer services that facilitate changing your account. It is less costly to switch to that bank, but more costly to switch *away* from it. This can be a successful strategy to build a loyal customer base.

Learning Costs

With many complex products such as enterprise resource planning or database software, extensive user learning is required to reap the full benefits from it. This is also true with simpler office applications such as Word or WordPerfect. Most people need time and support from experts working with a new spreadsheet or word processing program to learn how it works. People typically become more effective in using software as they gain experience.

This brand-specific investment of time eventually leads to **switching costs caused by learning.** Learning may also involve how to customize a certain product or service to the user's specific needs. In the software industry, learning costs are typically much higher than license fees.

Switching to a different brand means that consumers have to relearn some of the important product functions. This relearning with Brand B what we already know how to accomplish with Brand A is what creates learning costs. When we speak of learning costs, what we really mean are switch-related relearning costs. In fairness, if Brand B can provide features that Brand A cannot, the learning curve does not constitute switching costs.

The impact of learning costs on a brand's competitive position can be tremendous. Consider the struggle of Sun's Star Office against Microsoft Office:

Microsoft has created a market in which switching costs due to relearning are higher than license fees. In a 2002 study, Gartner Group analyzed the cost for migrating from Microsoft Office to Sun's Star Office for a mid-sized company. The sample enterprise has 2,500 users with 30%, or 750, staying on Microsoft Office and the other 70 percent (1,750) moving to Star Office (see http://gartner 2002.hec.Ca/research/107800/107883/107883.html# Bottom%20Line).

According to Gartner, for this migration, fixed-cost project management will amount to $110K at the company level and $5K at the department level. Switching costs to the employee level are comprised of transaction costs, user relearning (including the time-consuming conversion of old files), and license fees for each PC.

Total migration costs were estimated at $1,000 (best case) and $2,500 (worst case) per user. In this case this amounts to a staggering $2 mill to $4.5 mill in total switching costs. Consider that even under Microsoft's new price model ("License 6.0"), a new Office Suite license costs $350 against $35 for Star Office. Even in the best-case scenario, switching is three times as expensive as a new Microsoft Office license. Sun could give away Star Office for free and it wouldn't change much. Migration cannot possibly pay off.

Gartner concludes: "Software acquisition costs may only be the 'tip of the iceberg' compared with migration and learning costs. Ongoing costs of managing a diverse office automation environment should also be considered. Very casual users with relatively little interaction with users who may exchange more complex documents will be the best candidates for this project."

Most Microsoft Office Suite users are very loyal. They do their math. In unit sales, Microsoft holds a market share in the Office Suite market of 90%. Sun wants a market share of 10% by the end of 2003. As Gartner concludes, this can only come from "light" users with low switching costs and little or no need for converting files. There will be some, but it is obvious that the bulk of users are locked-in. The only help for Sun can come from substantially reducing switching costs for Microsoft Office users. Automatic and costless conversion of documents and other files is paramount. The relearning must be essentially zero.

Learning-induced switching costs also apply to commercial airlines with regard to their fleet management. FedEx, for example, has a very homogenous fleet of aircraft. Of its more than 650 airplanes, more than 600 are Boeing 727s. FedEx owns only a few other types such as Lockheed MD11 and Boeing 747. Southwest Airlines and Ryanair, both famous for efficient operations, fly only Boeing 737s.

Moving from a homogenous fleet of aircraft to a heterogeneous fleet creates substantial switching costs. Pilots, maintenance personnel, and flight attendants must be trained and certified for new types of aircraft. An airline's spare parts inventory increases, directly translating into higher costs per passenger seat mile.

It is no surprise that competitor Airbus has difficulty selling planes to customers with Boeing-only fleets. Airbus must compensate the airline for the switching costs, because the planes do not differ much in quality. When Airbus "sold" the first A-300 in the United States to Eastern Airlines back in the 1980s, rumor has it that it was given away at an enormous discount.

Recently, China Eastern Airlines ordered the first Airbus 320 jets. Airbus hopes to sell another 50 to China Eastern within the next years. Before that, Airbus invested $80 mill in a customer support and training center in Beijing to reduce the learning costs of China Eastern. Very recently Airbus reduced its list price by 60% to win a first order from all-Boeing EasyJet[5].

It is interesting that once learning costs are spent, they may not have to be spent again. Learning costs occur only when switching for the first time. Once China Eastern has A-320 jets, increasing their number will be less costly. This is because learning involves fixed costs such as the Airbus training center in Beijing.

This phenomenon may motivate customers to create strategic flexibility by consciously investing in learning, using different types of airplanes or software simultaneously. This can be seen in the IT department of larger corporations or universities, where some people are creating a Linux know-how pool. The goal is to facilitate a possible shift from Windows to Linux. Analogous, China Eastern values its increasing independency from Boeing higher than the switching costs created by buying aircraft from Airbus, specifically if Airbus shoulders part of the switching costs.

Loyalty Reward Programs

Loyalty reward programs are one of the most successful marketing instruments of the last 20 years. Frequent flyer programs rewarding frequent users with bonus points are the most prominent example.

Since the introduction of Advantage by American Airlines in 1981, frequent flyer programs (FFP) have been a crucial marketing instrument for airlines. FFP and similar programs provide

---

5 Source: "The Airbus has landed," Sunday Times, 10/20/2002, p. 6.

benefits to participants who consolidate their air travel mileage into a single FFP account. Benefits mostly come in the form of free additional flights or upgrades on regularly booked flights. Many airlines now offer a wide array of benefits in cooperation with several partners such hotel chains and car rental agencies.

The decision regarding which FFP to join is simple. Timothy Winship's acclaimed www.frequentflier.com consumer service website gives this advice:

> "You can't expect to consolidate mileage-earning in an FFP which doesn't meet your travel needs. And since most miles are earned for airline flights, the choice of FFP comes down to the choice of airline which best meets your travel needs. Over the long run, that will be the airline with the most flights from/to your home airport.
>
> "For example, if you live in Minneapolis, you will be flying mostly on Northwest . . . no matter what your final destination may be, and for that matter, no matter what your opinion of Northwest. Why? Because Northwest operates almost 80% of the flights into/out of the Minneapolis-St. Paul airport" (see http://www.frequentflier.com /ffp-006.htm).

Selection of the best FFP depends only on the number of miles participants will accumulate in the future, not necessarily on the quality of the service offered. Often, choice comes down to one or maybe two airlines frequently servicing a consumer's home airport. Most frequent travelers not located near a major airport serviced by several airlines face a monopoly even before entering an FFP.

FFPs are basically price discount programs based on accumulated consumption of a certain brand. They differ in sophistication, but not in principle, from Green Stamps or cigarette coupons. Participants receive higher discounts or benefits with more accumulated purchases. These benefits are purely contractual, as they are unrelated to transactional switching costs or learning costs.

A loyalty reward program can produce a strong lock-in effect, because switching from one airline to another leads to forsaken benefits. Switching airlines means not being able to accumulate travel miles. Here is an example.

> Suppose you have accumulated 23,000 miles with the FFP of airline A. For your next flight, two airlines (A and B) offer acceptable service and both offer 3,000 travel miles for their

FFP. Not switching means to increase the account with A to 26,000 miles, making you eligible for a free continental return ticket of your choice. Switching means you have to wait for that benefit until you fly with either A or B again. There is more of an immediate benefit to flying with airline A.

In practice, the issue becomes sometimes more difficult. Miles and benefits can expire. Additionally, airlines offer bonus programs with increased miles for certain promotion flights. This may complicate the optimal earning and spending of honor miles, but it does not change the idea.

Lock-in effects results if you are a member of only one FFP or, in case that you participate in several FFPs, your accumulated frequent flyer miles differ greatly among them. Then, switching costs occur as in the example above.

It is critical for customer lock-in that miles or points awarded for loyalty lose their value *outside* a certain loyalty reward program. You cannot profitably use Advantage miles to buy a Northwest Airlines ticket. This makes consolidation of air travel miles a brand-specific investment.

This doesn't mean that you cannot convert miles between FFPs although airlines try very hard to discourage that. Usually fliers don't convert their miles. Companies such as Honors Reward Exchange, Points.Com and Diners Club offer conversion services.[6] As market-makers, they make the conversion prices for miles. Not surprisingly, the conversion losses are significant. For example, Honors allows the exchange of 10,000 AA miles into 1,500 Midwest miles (85% loss). Points.Com exchanges 10,000 AA miles into 1,064 Midwest miles (90% loss). With such losses, www .frequentflier.com advises only to change small miles balances that will likely never accumulate to qualify for an award ("orphan miles"), or endangered miles from airlines about to go out of business.

For loyalty reward programs to work from a marketing perspective, bonus points must be brand-specific. High conversion loss forces customers to be loyal or to forsake benefits. Low-cost inter-convertibility of points or miles reduces the loyalty effect.

---

6 Source: http://www.smarterliving.com/columns/joy/column.php?id= 4618.

Brand-specific Investment

Accumulating purchases of a certain brand to receive loyalty rewards is a special case of brand-specific investment. Brand-specific investment also includes investment into "hard assets," such as:

- *proprietary technology* that induces loyalty with follow-up purchases for compatibility reasons (textbook example: video game consoles and game cartridges)
- supplier-specific investment into optimized supply-chain *procedures* (e.g., IT-based order systems)
- *site-specific* investment (for example, co-located production facilities)
- personal *relationships* with members of the supplier's organization
- emotional brand-specific bonds

Investments into personal relationships or emotional bonds to brands are sometimes considered "soft assets." They are often crucial for supplier-customer or brand-customer relationships to be sustainable. They provide the basis for the development of trust between the partners. However, compared to "hard assets" they sometimes play a minor role. Empirical research indicates that customers are more likely to abandon good personal relationships than bear "hard" switching costs.[7]

> The ongoing legal dispute between AK Steel and General Motors is a case in point. After a lengthy period of unsuccessful negotiation between AK Steel (supplier) and GM (customer), AK Steel announced on 2/6/2003 that it would sue GM for contract violation and threatened to drop GM as a customer. AK Steel had been a major steel supplier to 15 GM car plants for many years. The parties were in disagreement as to who had to cover additional costs that AK Steel claimed were the result of additional quality requirements by GM. Interrupting the supply of steel would seriously hurt GM. There are massive switching costs involved since AK Steel couldn't be exchanged by GM on short notice. A GM spokeswoman commented: "As any just-in-time company, any interruption of supply would significantly interrupt our operation" (New York Times, 2/7/2003).

---

7 Source: C.C. Nielson: An Empirical Examination of Switching-Cost Investments in Business-to-Business Marketing Relationships, Journal of Business & Industrial Marketing, vol. 11, 1996, 38-60.

This is clear case of conflict between "hard" (measurable) switching costs and costs related to the deterioration of personal relationships. It is very unusual that a supplier to the car industry sought help from the courts. It indicated that "hard" economic issues had begun to supersede soft assets in this relationship.

Compatibility

The necessity of compatibility between purchases made at different points in time can create powerful switching costs. Consider the market for video game consoles and game cartridges. You need to buy a console, but you will also buy games. Some games you will buy right away, bundled with the console. Some you will buy later. Basically, you invest in a video game system that results from a sequence of purchases.

Game cartridges are system-specific. A Nintendo cartridge won't fit into a Sega console or an X-Box, and vice-versa. This creates a compatibility problem. After buying a console, the customer faces lock-in with future purchases of complements. The same principle applies to printer supplies or certain spare parts for automobiles.

For the customer, it makes sense to stick to a certain system (for example, Nintendo), once committed to it by buying the console. Without games, the console is worthless. The more games purchased, the more users tend to commit to the initial investment. That means a higher likelihood of buying further components (new games) from the same supplier. One alternative is to buy a Sega console for Sega games. The price of this Sega console represents full switching cost because the consumer already has a Nintendo console.

Thus, consumers may not switch to another system. The higher the initial investment, the higher the pressure to "stick" to it. After some time buyers will rethink their system decision. This might happen when the initial investment is written off or considered obsolete. There is a strong lock-in effect coming from the urge to buy what is compatible with previous purchases.

The difference between compatibility-related switching costs and learning or transactional switching costs is that suppliers manipulate them through pricing. It depends on the price for a console—maybe together with a game—how high the switching costs are that the consumer must bear. If manufacturers give them away, there are no switching costs. The more expensive, the higher the switching costs.

With compatibility there is a tradeoff between creating a market with locked-in customers and exploiting them. High console prices lead to smaller markets with high exploitation value. Small console prices lead to bigger markets with a lower exploitation value. We will get back to this problem when discussing the economics of switching costs.

WHAT IS THE ESSENCE?

For more than 10 years now, the customer relationship concept has attracted significant interest by marketing professionals. Relationship Marketing Guru Jagdish Sheth of Emory University defines relationship marketing as "reduced choice." For example, the consumer reduces his set of relevant brands or suppliers. Stronger relationships provide more benefits than having more options. Reduced choice is the consumer's preference. A substantial part of the discussion in this area is concerned with providing superior product and service quality to create and sustain brand preference. With switching costs, the consumer's preference is only relevant *before* the purchase decision and *before* vendor-specific investment is made. After switching costs arise, customer preference becomes less relevant. This is a significant difference to the relationship marketing concept. Switching costs can create hostages who prefer shopping somewhere else.

Switching costs for customers result from different sources. Some are unavoidable, such as certain types of transactional switching costs or learning costs. Therefore, some companies offer discounts to first-time customers in order to reduce switching costs to them. Other types of switching costs are created by the company. Company-induced switching costs can be caused by brand-specific learning or compatibility issues with streams of purchases into a system. They can also be created by offering loyalty awards that are valuable (only) inside that relationship.

Switching costs created by a company are sometimes called artificial. This indicates that companies have some discretion in designing contracts with customers and that this discretion involves the creation of switching costs. Creating artificial switching costs can be a powerful marketing instrument to increase the loyalty of the customer base.

With regard to personal relationships between customer and vendor, it seems that the power of trust and emotion as a bond to brands and suppliers is overrated. If profitable, buyers are ready to abandon good personal relationships with previous suppliers. This is not limited to B2B marketing. Managers of many consumer brands see that every day. Thinking about proprietary technology or loyalty reward programs seems to be more interesting.

3

The Economics of Switching Costs: Where's the Beef?

Management is about achieving profits. More specifically, it is about competitive advantage to achieve above-normal profits. Normal profits are the average profit level in your industry. "Above normal" means that your company performs better than average. To achieve profits requires a competitive advantage.

Firms try to achieve a competitive advantage through product and process innovation. Even if successful, most quality and cost advantages are more or less short-lived. Innovative and successful strategies are subject to imitation. In some industries, imitation is fast because of the lack of imitation barriers (for example, airlines, hotels). In others, it is slower, for example, because of patent protection (as in the pharmaceutical industry). Rarely does it happen that new and successful concepts leading to competitive advantage are not imitated. Innovation followed by imitation lies at the heart of Joseph Schumpeter's widely acclaimed theory of economic development.

A customer base with significant switching costs is a resource that cannot be quickly imitated by competitors. Sun had to learn this lesson the hard way with Linux and Star Office. Both software products are essentially free. For many users, however, price doesn't even come close to their switching costs. The forced loyalty of Microsoft customers is a resource that is very hard to imitate. Interestingly, this advantage is independent from product differentiation or cost advantages that Sun's software might have.

Only a valuable resource such as a locked-in customer base that cannot be imitated provides a sustainable competitive advantage. A locked-in customer base is such a resource. This is the reason why it is paramount to understand the economics of switching costs. Today, there is an immense body of research on switching costs. So far, it has had little impact on discussion in management and marketing. If it has, it comes from economists such as Carl Shapiro and Hal Varian at Berkeley (their excellent book *Information Rules* is a good example) or Paul Klemperer from Oxford, who has contributed significantly to conceptual research on switching costs.

In this section we will look at the economics of switching costs. One of the most important results is that switching costs can create potential for companies to increase prices for "old" (for example, locked-in) customers. This does not necessarily mean that markets with switching costs are not competitive or that average profit levels are always higher. It does mean that significant potential for higher profits exists if the switching cost game is played right.

SWITCHING COSTS: THE CUSTOMER EQUITY DRIVER

Switching costs increase the retention rate of a customer base and increase the probability to cross- and up-sell to customers. Thus, switching costs strongly affect customer equity. Here is a simple example to demonstrate why.[1]

Consider the case of internet service providers (ISPs). They have little potential for sustainable product differentiation. Any differentiation advantage is quickly imitated. Customers, however, develop switching costs due to provider-specific learning. Therefore, to encourage customers to switch, ISPs routinely offer price discounts (for example, AOL's "free 45 days trial").[2]

Consider this simple model:

A customer will switch from ISP A to B, if the present value of switching exceeds the present value of staying with ISP A. Let us assume a simple two period model with two ISPs in which prices p are identical for ISPs and do not change over time. Customers who switch receive a discount d (measured in $) on the first period price, but must bear switching cost s. Thus, their first period price is $(p - d + s)$. In the case of AOL, $p - d$ is zero for 1.5 months.

If the market is highly competitive, customers have no preference for ISPs. Both provide the same benefits. Customers will switch if

$$(p - d) + \frac{p}{r} + s < p + \frac{p}{r}$$

---

1 This example was taken from: C. Shapiro and H. Varian: Note to accompany Information Rules, available at http://www.inforules.com/models/m-switch.pdf.
2 Compared to airlines it's the other way around: Customers receive an initial discount only to pay higher regular prices later.

with r as the interest rate to calculate the present value of the second period price.

This condition says that switching is cheaper than staying over both periods. Since both ISPs offer the same benefits, the present value of switching to B is higher. Consumers are indifferent between switching and staying if this condition holds:

$$(p - d) + \frac{p}{r} + s = p + \frac{p}{r}$$

Second period costs are the same for both ISPs and, thus, irrelevant in this model. It follows that:

$$(p - d) + s = p \quad \text{or} \quad d = s$$

In a highly competitive market without brand preference (consumers don't really care which ISP they use), the discount offered exactly equals the switching costs. Or in other words: You wouldn't offer higher discounts than customer switching costs.

This result depends on the assumption that the market is highly competitive and that customers are homogeneous and have no brand preference. With some markets, however, this comes quite close to reality. For example, competition on many domestic and international airline routes is fierce. It has been hotly debated whether frequent flyer miles are a sign of ferocious price competition. Paul Klemperer argues that this is actually not the case—his analysis points out that FFPs lead to discounts on prices which, in the absence of discounts, would be even lower.[3]

Look at the profit implications of our simple model. In a highly competitive industry, profits are small. Any profit advantage will be competed away quickly. To simplify modeling, we assume that profits are not possible. Then:

$$(p - c) - s + \frac{p - c}{r} = 0 \quad \text{or} \quad (p - c) + \frac{p - c}{r} = s$$

with c as total costs per period. Note that

$$(p - c) + \frac{p - c}{r}$$

is the net present value (or customer equity) of each customer. The result is that customer equity equals switching costs.

---

3 See P. Klemperer: Markets with Switching Costs, The Quarterly Journal of Economics, May 1987, 377–394.

You might think this model is too simple to explain reality. Consider the following example from the airlines industry.

FFP pioneer American Airlines offers 5,222 bonus miles for a non-stop round-trip flight from Boston to Los Angeles. At American's website www.aa.com, the Logan-LAX round-trip airfare is $476. To collect sufficient miles for a free continental round-trip (25,000 miles with PlanAhead), customers must fly this route 5 times or spend a total of $2,380 in order to receive a discount of $476 on the 6th flight. This makes an AAdvantage mile worth $0.018 ($476/[5*5,222]). Accordingly, the bonus mileage of each trip is worth $95.20.

The regular round-trip ticket from Boston to Los Angeles should cost $380.80 if American's FFP did not exist ($476 – $95.20). Consumers pay ticket prices that are up to *25% higher* in order to receive discounts later—after another 4 flights. It is obvious why this program boosts customer equity.

- Most travelers pay "full fare" ($476 in our example). Usually there are only a few options for "mileage-free" tickets. Airlines may offer specials or promotions with no FFP mileage attached. But these promotions are not widely available for every time or for every route. The promotions are also subject to substantial restrictions.[4] Infrequent travelers are forced to pay the premium of $95.20 and feed the FFP program with orphan miles even though they cannot expect to receive discounts.
- Many frequent travelers have switching costs (the miles you already have and wish to use). They provide a strong incentive to be loyal even in the event of substantially higher prices.
- Compared to ISPs or printer manufacturers, airlines use switching costs the clever way—consumers must pay higher prices up front in order to receive a (possible) discount later. This is a nice way of cash fast-forwarding.
- In practice, the discount you receive (a free ticket for a number of bonus miles) does not equal the switching cost, but is less than that. Airlines get more than they give because every airline has substantial costs to manage its FFP. Investment for an FFP can cost in the triple million dollar area. A proper return on this investment is expected. Effectively, the discount is reduced to earn that return.

---

4 As of April 2, 2003, American Airlines offered a $249 round-trip fare from Boston to Los Angeles. This special offer is subject to many restrictions (limited seating, tickets nonrefundable, etc.).

- Most importantly, airlines limit the availability of discounts to where it hurts less or not at all. Getting a free ticket for a popular route at peak time is difficult or even impossible. As a rule of thumb, around 5% of the seats on each flight are given away on the basis of bonus miles. If it would be more, bonus mile passengers would start to compete with regular passengers. As an airline, you don't want that. What you want is getting the bonus traveler on a less crowded route or on the plane at off-peak time with no marginal costs.

Airlines have looked very closely into the impact of switching costs on customer equity. It is not surprising that they discovered proper FFP management to increase customer loyalty and willingness-to-pay at the same time. But they have also developed sophisticated instruments to control the costs of that system. Both capabilities are essential.

Two results are noteworthy.

1. Airline customers pay ticket prices that include the financial benefit from the frequent flyer miles they receive after using the ticket—in other words, there is no such thing as a free lunch.
2. The higher switching costs are for the customer, the higher is the customer's worth to the airline.

MAKING PRICE DISCRIMINATION FEASIBLE

One of most striking effects of switching costs is that they allow vendors to price discriminate effectively between different types of customers. Marketers have always been in love with price discrimination. Price discrimination (PD) basically means that you sell the same product at different prices to different types of customers with different willingness-to-pay. In a market with heterogeneous customers, it is the only way to maximize profits.[5]

Price discrimination can be implemented in various forms that differ in their impact on profits.

1. Perfect price discrimination ("first degree") occurs if a vendor charges exactly what each customer is willing to pay, similar to what happens in a bazaar. Although compelling in theory, it is very hard to implement outside the bazaar. Customers don't

---

5 For an excellent overview on the theory of price discrimination, see J. Tirole: The Theory of Industrial Economics, MIT Press 1997.

want to be charged their individual willingness-to-pay, but less than that, if possible. So they don't want to disclose what they think a product or service is worth.

The closest to perfect price discrimination in reality is an auction of rare products, for example, a Van Gogh painting or a mobile phone network license. There is little or no chance to buy the same item later. The bidder is forced to disclose his or her true willingness-to-pay in a competitive situation to have a chance to win.

Recently, this very effective auction model has seen a broader implementation through on-line marketplaces such as eBay. eBay offers a very attractive model to sell goods and services because it puts competing buyers in a situation in which they have to disclose their willingness-to pay.[6]

2. Second-degree price discrimination is applied if vendors have no information about the preferences of individual customers, but know that different types of customers exist. They will then design specific products for different types and allow customers to choose according to their preferences. The idea is that customers buy what suits them best. In economic theory, this is called "self selection."

Self selection is often used in the marketing of consumer goods. It is impractical to obtain information about every possible customer. And it would be naïve to believe that customers disclose their willingness-to-pay if they are not forced to do so. It is much more efficient to discover customer preferences through their actual purchasing behavior. Many companies have implemented second-degree PD through product variation targeted at multiple market segments. Some are very successful.[7]

---

6 To be exact, eBay's auction process extracts the second highest bidders' willingness-to-pay and not that of the winner. This holds for every "classic" auction process in which bids go up (the so-called "English Auction"). The moment the last co-bidder leaves the auction the winner is determined. This happens at the highest price that this co-bidder is willing to pay. The winner wins the auction by adding the smallest possible monetary value to this bid. In order to extract the willingness-to-pay of the highest bidder, prices must go down ("Dutch Auction"). In this type of auction, the first to raise his hand is the winner.

7 One of the most prominent examples is the breakfast cereals industry with key players Kellogg, General Mills and Kraft Foods. Margins in this industry are 3-4 times higher than in other packaged food sectors. This is because product differentiation proliferates. Kellogg, Kraft and "the General" have more than 120 different types of cereals on the market. Virtually every consumer type (differentiated by age, dietary needs, preferences, health consciousness) is covered. This creates micro-segments in which customers are loyal and willingness-to-pay can be extracted. No brand has a market share of more than 4%.

The problem with this approach, and the reason it produces less profit than perfect price discrimination, is that customers are free to buy products not intended for them. A typical business traveler may fly coach because coach service has been improved. Economists call this phenomenon *arbitrag* to describe customers who don't purchase what or where they are supposed to. Since customers can choose freely, they may switch between segments. In the business traveler's case, it means that an airline's ability to extract true willingness-to-pay is limited. Some of the business traveler's willingness-to-pay is lost by arbitrage when the offering for lower segments improves.

3. Third-degree PD is based on a customer attribute observable to the vendor. A typical example is price discrimination between different age groups. For example, VIA Rail Canada offers a 10% discount and a free ticket for one travel companion to passengers 60 years and older. Other examples are discounts for young children at the movies or higher college tuition for out-of-state students.

    If the segment an individual customer belongs to can be identified, price can be set accordingly. Price is determined by each segment's elasticity of demand. The lower its price elasticity, the higher is the price charged in that segment.

    With third-degree PD, "observability" of segment membership is crucial. A form of identification can be used to verify age. The same holds for students. But preferences or willingness-to-pay are not observable traits and customers have a strong incentive to cheat. Price discrimination is usually based on an observable attribute.

Switching costs may allow for effective third-degree PD between new and old customers. Old customers bear switching costs because they have made vendor-related purchases in the past and are locked-in with regard to related purchases. New customers have not yet made a commitment to a supplier or brand (or perceive that commitment as obsolete), and are free of switching cost.

Often vendors can identify old customers through their purchasing behavior. Customers buy complement parts such as printing supplies, spare parts, or video game cartridges. New customers are in the market for the initial investment such as printers or game consoles, possibly bundled with some complements. This can be a very effective basis to price discriminate, as the HP case demonstrates.

We have already discussed the monopoly power that switching costs bring. Together with the potential for price discrimination, this creates a strong incentive to act as a monopolist against the customer base. Because the demand elasticity of old customers is lower, prices will be higher for them.

In economics literature, is has been pointed out that with compatibility-induced switching costs, vendors influence the degree to which old and new customers can be priced differently.[8] Again, the game console industry is a good example. If Nintendo would give away consoles for free, there would be no switching costs. If a person fancies a new game from a different system, he just gets a new console. The switch is more costly when consoles are more expensive. Higher console prices increase the vendor's ability to price discriminate against old customers when buying games.

Price discrimination against old customers comes at a cost. This cost refers to the supplier's ability to attract new customers. A printer buyer may check the price of printing supplies with various brands *before* a new printer is bought and then buy a more expensive printer if the total costs of ownership are lower.

In general, extensive price discrimination against the customer base reduces the chances to expand that base. This may be an irrelevant issue to a dominant industry player (for example, Microsoft or Oracle) with little remaining potential to enlarge its customer base. However, it may be very relevant to a start-up company.

> With that in mind, it becomes clear what Microsoft is doing with its new pricing policy ("License 6.0"). Microsoft as a large player can profitably act as a monopolist against the installed base of customers. Microsoft easily identifies these old customers through the purchasing of complements. In this case, these are upgrades on software packages. Old customers are now left with two choices: They can buy a new license or they can choose a plan under which they have to purchase every update that is released.

SWITCHING COSTS AND ETHICS: A DILEMMA?

This book is not a treatise of ethical dilemmas that may arise in markets with switching costs. Switching costs are an important

---

8 See: B.G. Mari_oso: Technological Incompatibility, Endogenous Switching Costs and Lock-in, *The Journal of Industrial Economics*, vol. 49, September 2001, 281-300.

driver of customer loyalty and they may be so high that customers are forced to use a certain supplier for a long time against their preference, becoming an economic hostage. Theory suggests that in this situation the customer's price elasticity of demand is very low. Logic demands that prices must be higher for that type of customer to maximize profits. This is referred to as "price discrimination against old customers."

Is price discrimination against old customers unethical? Should companies take advantage of their customers being hostages? The answer to this question is yes, with the following explanation.

- Customers are rational and they anticipate lock-in. For example, database software buyers are clever enough to realize that making full use of such a complex product requires a lot of training for a lot of employees. Extensive brand-specific training presents a burden to change to another supplier before the initial investment has paid off. Because they see a lock-in coming, they will select suppliers or brands that are less risky. Competition will produce efficient bundles of product quality, price and switching costs.
- If price discrimination against old customers is wrong or unethical, then all other ways of discriminating against customer types are unethical as well. How can we tell which way of price discrimination is okay? Price discrimination is necessary for many companies to survive. If airlines could not discriminate against business travelers, how could the airlines generate a profit? Consumers have come to accept price discrimination. Moviegoers accept discounts for young children at the theater. Consumers accept that there are different class sections in an airplane. Most people have never flown first class, because it's too expensive. This does not motivate them to start a crusade against airlines due to excessive price discrimination against business travelers. Markets work in the sense that because established national airlines have discriminated too much, new no-frills players such as Southwest Airlines have entered the arena, driving prices down.
- Markets are efficient, even with switching costs. Price discrimination can only occur in the second period (when companies have "old customers"). If companies offer first period discounts to attract new customers, it does not necessarily mean that average prices and overall profits are higher. In

some markets, the contrary is the case. Low entry pricing to build a base of locked-in customers—who are supposed to pay higher prices later—can be a negative-sum game. We will get back to this problem in part 3 (chapter 9).

- Rational customers that are aware of lock-in problems before their initial investment will look at the probability of being exploited by a supplier. This means that a company's reputation plays a crucial role. Reputation is the sum the other buyers experience with that company. If companies start to exploit customers by excessive price discrimination, it will be very hard to attract new customers. This means that in efficient markets the potential for opportunistic price discrimination is limited. This issue will be discussed in more depth in part 4 (chapter 13).

Do markets with switching costs present ethical dilemmas? Yes, but these dilemmas are not new or special. Companies can try to conceal what amount of brand-specific investment is necessary. They can lie and cheat, break contracts, excessively raise prices and so on. All this is possible and it happens, but it is by no means limited to markets with switching costs.

If markets are efficient (and they should be) and customers are rational, then markets with switching costs do not present unique ethical problems.

SUMMARY OF PART I

Customer lock-in is a strategy based on customer switching costs. Switching costs prevent customers from changing brands and suppliers whenever they want. In an age in which even highly satisfied customers defect, this is a compelling reason to think about the potential of a customer lock-in strategy.

Switching costs are not limited to specific industries. Their influence on loyalty and profits is pervasive in banking, in IT, in mobile phone services, and even in commodity markets, to name a few. Every industry presents opportunities to create switching costs.

Switching costs are a key driver of customer retention and the probability to cross- and up-sell to the customer base. They influence customer equity tremendously. A wise investment would be in companies that understand the economics of switching costs.

PART 2

Understanding Markets with Switching Costs

A strategy based on customer lock-in requires a thorough understanding of the forces in markets with switching costs. They change important elements of industry analysis and create specific strategy implementation hurdles. In this part we will look more closely at the following implications of strategies based on switching costs on the industry and the market level.

- *How do switching costs influence a customer's buying behavior? We must assume that customers are rational. This means they are aware of switching costs before they purchase.*
- *In relation to the previous item, the very important issue of customer acceptance of switching cost.*
- *The development of a switching cost-based model of market segmentation. This model provides insights into the structure of a market in terms of its accessibility. Companies in a switching-cost rich market must look not only at the sheer number of buyers and their demand, but also at the degree to which they are committed to other brands via switching costs.*
- *The development of marketing strategies based on different switching costs segments. This relates to the question of how to migrate customers.*
- *The influence of switching costs on customer equity. The certainty of future streams of revenues from customers is very much determined by the extent of individual switching costs.*

4

Who Wins the Game?

BIG IS BEAUTIFUL: THE BATTLE FOR MARKET SHARE

In markets with lock-in, market share becomes a strong indicator for tomorrow's profits. An even better indicator may be the installed base of customers. The customer base that a company has created is the foundation for higher profits achieved through price discrimination in the future. To what extent price discrimination is profitable is determined by the installed base the company has and the number of new customers left that will enter this market in the future.

The outlook of higher profits later provides a strong incentive to "buy" market share today. Pricing is one instrument, because aggressive pricing can enlarge the customer base. Or, as Shapiro and Varian put it, the vendor "invests in discounts to acquire a flow of markups in the future."

Again, a trade-off emerges. A vendor can trade today's profit (through lower prices to attract new customers) against tomorrow's profit (through higher prices from locked-in customers). This can be a zero-sum game. Whether it is or not largely depends upon what customers' expectations are and what type of customer is attracted by low "entry prices."

In his papers on this issue, Paul Klemperer has stressed that if customers are rational, they will expect lower prices today to be followed by higher prices tomorrow. This logic seems straightforward. However, the assumption is that customers anticipate their lock-in and the possibility of price increases or some other way of exploitation later on. If they do, they will be less sensitive to first period prices. Then customers understand that low first period prices are supposed to facilitate an initial investment that creates an unfavorable lock-in situation. Thus, lower first period prices may not have the intended effect, because they may not be successful in creating a large customer base.

In such a situation, pricing alone cannot create a substantial customer base. There must be additional benefits for customers to attach themselves to a certain supplier. Product and service attributes may be such benefits. In each case, the battle for market share will be fought on many fronts.

Many dotcoms believed that aggressive pricing ("follow the free") would greatly enhance their future market position. Basically, it was a run for market share through low first period pricing. The idea was to create a substantial customer base as soon as possible. The problem is that one day this customer base should be paying this company for something. It is amazing that many people at this time focused on market share alone, but not on the market share/price discrimination/profit link.

Switching costs can be such a link between market share and profit. This link, however, depends on the company's ability to eventually price discriminate against "old customers."

In the battle for market share, smaller competitors have a much stronger incentive for price competition than larger players. Smaller players can enlarge their customer base by cutting prices without hurting their revenues from their (smaller) customer base. Larger players, in contrast, have little incentive to cut prices because this hurts more with their larger customer base.

In a market with only a few but large players, there will be little price competition. Instead, it is more profitable to act "monopolistically against the customer base," as economists say. By that they mean to exploit them by raising prices. Only the existence of smaller competitors drives prices down.

For new and smaller comers to establish a customer base, it is critical to overcome customer switching costs. If these are high, this might turn out to be very difficult. Under lock-in, price loses its power to attract buyers. Remember Star Office's futile struggle against Microsoft: switching costs of professional Microsoft Office users range between $1,000 and $2,500. A Star Office Suite costs $35 against $350 for Microsoft Office. Even a price of *zero* would not help.

NETWORK EFFECTS: SWITCHING COSTS ON THE MARKET LEVEL

Markets with network effects are markets in which the benefit of a product to consumers increases with the number of users. They create a strong "desire for compatibility with other consumers' choices."[1] Telecommunication is a perfect example. A phone is more useful if more people have one. This phenomenon is called a *network externality*.

Markets with network externalities can "tip." Tipping describes a situation in which one brand that has a small initial market share advantage in early stages of market development will automatically increase its market share over time and eventually dominate the market. This happens because even a small initial market share advantage translates into higher benefits for each consumer. This motivates other consumers to buy this brand, creating a positive feedback loop. The market share increases, motivating even more consumers to buy this brand, and so forth.[2] At the end, a single brand survives. Because of the strong effect of the number of users on product benefits, there is no other possible outcome. It is "path dependent."

For path dependency and dominance of a single brand, the reason for a brand's initial market share advantage and its size is irrelevant. Case studies from several industries have shown that the dominating brand must not be the one with the highest quality (think about Sony's futile struggle with Betamax against Matsushita's VHS). Even "small" or seemingly insignificant events can tip a network market in favor of a single player.

The difference between switching costs and network effects is that with switching costs customers care about the compatibility of individual purchases, made one after the other. With network effects they care about the compatibility with purchases that others have made.

Markets with switching costs can be subject to network externalities. If you use certain word processing software and you exchange documents with other people, switching away from the standard reduces the compatibility of your output. Switching also comes about if consumers derive their expectations from the number of fellow brand-users. Expectations are important as we have seen with the power of first period pricing. If customers

---

1 See: J. Farrell and P. Klemperer: Coordination and Lock-In: Competition with Switching Costs and Network Effects, available at www.nuff.ox.ac.uk/users/klemperer/lockin-webversion.pdf, 2001.

2 In theoretical literature, this effect is known as path dependency. Once a brand in a market with network externalities has gained a market share advantage, this advantage must increase until domination. It does not matter how large this initial advantage is. For an excellent treatment of this issue, see: B. Arthur: Increasing Returns and Path Dependency in the Economy, The University of Michigan Press, 2000.

expect second period prices to rise, then the impact of smaller prices in the first period will be lower. Their "attraction value" is diminished.

Now, customers may expect second period prices to be lower if more (other) brand users exist. They may think that a company with a big installed user base has less incentive to "exploit share." This incentive may be stronger for a smaller player. A large user base also indicates that many other buyers came to the conclusion this vendor is one that will not excessively price discriminate. This also is a positive network effect.

THE ROLE OF COMPLEMENTS

A force that is extremely important in markets with switching costs is the complements to products or services. For example, application software is a complement to computer operating software. In general, complements are defined as "factors in which the increase of one factor increases the marginal value of the other."[3] From a product perspective, it is implied that complements are accessories to a certain technology or brand that enhance its value.

Application software is immensely valuable to operating system (OS) suppliers, because without applications an operating system is worthless. Complements boost the demand for the "original" product. Without application software, even the greatest OS dies. The same is true in the game console market in which the availability of games (complements) drives the demand for consoles. In industry practice, complements are the basis for price discrimination against the customer base.

The increasing importance of complements is due to the more and more integrated use of modern technology. For example, information technology, telecommunication technology, and multimedia applications are merging into a totally new field of services. Mobile phones are used in conjunction with laptops for mobile internet access, creating a wealth of new applications. The success of Napster is due to a new combination of complements—many music enthusiasts with internet access and digital music files to share, CD-RW drives, and a freely accessible internet-based exchange platform.

---

3 This definition was proposed by Edgeworth in 1938.

Wide availability of complements can create tremendous switching costs. Microsoft is good example. So much application software is available for Windows that customers are locked-in. Many users would never opt for Linux or OS/2 because there is less application software available.

When performing an industry analysis, pay close attention to where the industry is heading. A more integrated use of technologies and services by customers strongly hints at offerings and different brands becoming complements to each other. Look at what customers buy in bundles simultaneously compared to what they expect to purchase as complements later.

You should use the possibility of creating switching costs by motivating other companies to develop complements for your technology. SAP's overwhelming success in Germany and other countries is due to its success in partnering with many independent IT consultants who provide the critical implementation services for SAP's complex enterprise software. The same principle can make a company large in their industry.

WHAT IS THE ESSENCE?

Winning the customer lock-in game requires an understanding of the changes to the rules of competition. Market share and profit are highly correlated in markets with switching costs. Big players profit disproportionally from price discrimination against locked-in customers. Large companies have a larger customer base to profit from and they present high entry barriers to competitors. With a few big incumbents, there is little incentive to engage in price competition. High prices will be sustainable. Even a small market-share advantage tends to increase somewhat automatically when network externalities exist.

In the next chapter, we will look into the changes to buying behavior. Consumers' perceived risk plays a major role in brand selection. Risk results from the impending lock-in when adopting a certain brand. When many other consumers have adopted a certain brand, new buyers may think that the same choice is less risky. This is a network effect resulting in path dependency. Complements to products and services (accessories) are the basis of generating profit from your locked-in customer base. They are often bought after the initial brand choice is made. In that situation, you are a monopolist.

Even considering these factors, it is still possible to overcome the dominant market position of a company like Microsoft with a huge installed base of heavily locked-in customers. Innovation can lead to superior benefits that may surpass high switching costs. It requires creative destruction.

5

Changes to Buying Behavior

Analyzing buying behavior and market segmentation are necessary to understand the structure of your market. In a market with switching costs, it is very important to know which customers are unlikely to switch and why.

The market segmentation concept presented later will focus on brand performance advantage to compensate for the risks customers incur when switching brands. A somewhat simplified approach, it neglects the possibility that customers actively implement strategies to reduce the risk when switching brands.

We need to look more closely at the issue of customers' purchasing behavior in the event of switching costs. Switching costs put customers at risk because of lock-in. Rational customers anticipate lock-in. They are aware of switching costs and their consequences, and they will try to avoid lock-in traps.

In the public discussion of switching costs, they are sometimes described as "hidden or unanticipated costs of switching from one technology or brand to another."[1] This implies that customers become aware of switching costs only after it is too late—and are then exploited by opportunistic suppliers. In reality this might happen, but it's a dangerous assumption to build a strategy on. Instead, assume that customers are aware of looming lock-in problems.

Customers can avoid lock-in or its possible negative consequences by either reducing the amount of brand-specific investment or by insuring it (see Figure 5-1). The idea of reducing brand-specific investment is simple: Customers try to receive the same benefits without investing heavily into brand idiosyncrasies. For example, in the software industries, some companies promote their brands as "minimal install" technology.[2]

Alternatively, customers can try to insure their brand-specific investment. Insuring means to implement some measure that

---

1 See: http://www.cbi.cgey.com/journal/issue3/features/inforule/.
2 See for example: http://digitalsmarties.com/services.html.

reduces the severity of the loss in case the unwanted event occurs. This measure can be the contract with the vendor, the customer's ability to effect his reputation, or dual sourcing.

Figure 5-1 shows an overview.

INSURING BRAND-SPECIFIC INVESTMENT

A supplier doesn't want customers to reduce lock-in by offering "minimal install" technology. Lock-in is vital to the establishment of a profitable customer base. Thus, reducing lock-in is always an inferior strategy to insuring it. Insuring means to provide some counterweight against the unwanted effects of customer lock-in. Insurance can be provided in different ways: through the contract, by reputation, or dual sourcing.

Contractual Insurance

Contractual agreements can be a powerful source of insurance for customers against the unwanted effects of lock-in. Contractual insurance is provided by clauses in the contract that prohibit or demand certain vendor behavior.

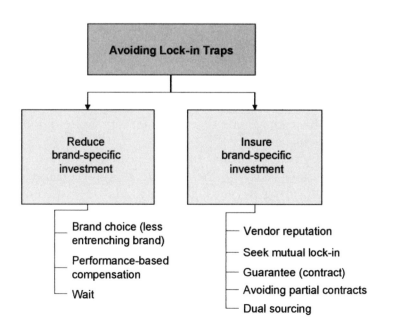

Figure 5-1. Customer Strategies to Avoid Lock-in Traps

The vendor can be required by contract to make updates for his software available on a regular basis or regulate that prices for complements are not excessive. Customers' ability to implement such contracts depends on their position in relation to the supplier. The more powerful and indispensable customers are to suppliers, the more contractual insurance they can demand.

Contractual insurance implements mutual lock-in. Mutual lock-in requires the vendor to specifically invest in the customer. A counterweight is created that keeps both parties interested in an ongoing and productive relationship.

Here is a typical situation in the auto industry. The German car manufacturer Audi operates two plants in Germany, one in Ingolstadt (where the smaller A3 and A4 are produced), and another in Neckarsulm (where the larger sedans are assembled). To keep inventory costs down, many suppliers have moved production into the vicinity of both plants. Among them is Faurecia, a French seat manufacturer.

To become the sole supplier of seats for the A3 and A4 models, Faurecia had to open a plant in Neuburg, a small town 15 miles to the north east of Ingolstadt. From there, Faurecia delivers complete seating packages (front seats and the rear seat bench) built-to-order with a lead time of only 4 hours.

Since all car makers want that flexibility in production, the Neuburg plant is worthless to Faurecia if it loses the Audi account. Also, JIT delivery with a lead time of 4 hours cannot be duplicated by any other seat maker on short notice. Thus, both partners are locked in. Audi experiences strong lock-in because there is no other seat maker available to deliver the right seats on short notice. For Audi, this is a risky arrangement. Interruption at Faurecia would cause production standstill for Audi's A3 and A4 models within hours, and would cost millions of dollars per day. Theoretically, this kind of arrangement might cause Faurecia to become lax in its pursuit to deliver quality to Audi.

Audi needs mutual lock-in to insure that risk. This is implemented by forcing any seat supplier (Faurecia in this case) to manufacture locally. Faurecia's local plant at Neuburg is to a large extent worthless if Faurecia loses the Audi account.

Thus, local investment at Neuburg is partly specific to Audi. Because of that, Audi's threat of eventually changing seat suppliers is powerful.

What you have here is an "equilibrium of terror." Any attempt to exploit a partner's lock-in will possibly result in retaliation. It's effective insurance against the unwanted effects of lock-in.

In general, customers will try to avoid partial contracts. A partial contract leaves too much leeway to the supplier. A supplier may or may not use that leeway to increase profits at the customer's cost after the customer is locked-in.

Confronted with customers who try to avoid lock-in, a company can opt for a reactive or an active contracting strategy. A reactive strategy means to wait for the customer to signal a wish to negotiate for more insurance in the contract. If that signal doesn't come, a company offers a standard contract with as little mutual lock-in as possible. Being active means to offer different types of contracts with different levels of insurance at different prices, and then let customers self-select.

The active strategy is superior for two reasons. First, it gives those customers who might be put off by your standard contract offering a chance to negotiate. Such potential customers would be lost right away without that chance. Second, it always pays to differentiate a product in a market with heterogeneous customers. Like Goldilocks, customers want what feels "just right." As customers differ, so will their preferred contractual arrangement. If various arrangements are offered up front, transaction costs are saved all around.

Even in a highly heterogeneous market, two to three different types of contracts with increasing levels of insurance suffice. From a profitability standpoint, a company doesn't need a different contract for every customer. Negotiating an individual contract is very costly. Implementing individual contracts often adds excessive fulfillment costs. This quickly eats up the additional revenues from more differentiation.

In order to make self-selection work, substantial differentiation between the low end (no or little insurance) and the high end (complete mutual lock-in) is necessary. Position the "in between" contract a little closer to the higher end than the low end to extract additional willingness-to-pay from the majority of somewhat risk-averse buyers who don't value the two extremes.

But don't lose sight of the most important issue, profit from providing additional insurance. If customers are insured against risk from lock-in, they experience additional value. A company needs to be sure to get adequately paid for adding value. If not, it should look for other instruments to attract risk-averse buyers.

Vendor Reputation

Contracts can never be all-encompassing instruments to insure customer risk resulting from customer lock-in. Contracts are always incomplete. It's difficult to foresee everything that happens in the future, therefore, it is impossible to hedge all risks by contract design.

If some risk remains, who does the customer turn to? The answer is simple—a company that has a good reputation as being diligent and following up on its promises.

A good reputation reflects on a vendor's past behavior. It is the outcome of word-of-mouth communication in the market. Consumers tend to extrapolate information received from third parties into the future. For example, if a company has honored its promises in the past, consumers assume that it will honor them in the future, too.[3]

This assumption may be wrong. Reputation can only function as insurance for brand-specific investment if any customer can damage the vendor's reputation by word-of-mouth so much that *many* other customers will refrain from doing business with the company. These "spillover effects" are crucial.[4] The more spillover effects occur, the more reputation will be an effective safeguard against opportunism. For fast and far-reaching spillover effects, an efficient communication system is needed.

> For example, western democracies have quite efficient communication systems. There is little friction in getting information out and creating spillover effects. This is the reason why the U.S. federal government honored a fisheries contract with Canada, which after signing turned out to be rather disadvantageous, in order to secure cooperation with Japan on defense policy.

---

3 There is an extensive body of literature on reputation and its role in economic theory. Examples include the paper by Kreps and Wilson (1982) or Herbig, Milewicz and Golden (1994).
4 See Cole, H.L. and Kehoe, P.J. (1996): Reputation Spillover across Relationships: Reviving Reputation Models of Debt, NBER Working Paper Nr. 5486.

Reputation is effective insurance for brand-specific investment if an exploited customer can significantly hurt the vendor's chances to do business with other customers.

How can a company use its reputation to motivate potential customers to lock-in to its brand? A company can motivate exploited customers to bad-mouth it and provide simple and easy-to-use instruments that create a lot of spillover effects. If that idea seems bizarre, think again. Reputation is worth nothing to customers as insurance if they can't hurt it. If there is no platform for communication between customers, or if communication is very costly, reputation can't work as insurance.

Some software companies such as Cisco operate bug bulletins on the internet for its products. Anyone can look into them and find out about problems encountered by users, and how the supplier handled the problems. This open approach levels the playing field for everyone. It's not a matter of size for a customer to be heard, because every user can post his problems. Everybody sees how the supplier reacted and when. With this method, the internet substitutes whatever formal and informal communication networks between customers have previously been necessary. It is a good example for suppliers facilitating communication between customers.

The more companies help customers in exchanging information, the more reputation can serve as insurance of brand-specific investment. It is an impressive signal that the vendor is highly motivated to keep promises.

Dual Sourcing

Dual sourcing introduces competition between specialized suppliers and therefore reduces customer lock-in. Here is an example.

In April 2001, Motorola signed a contract with California-based chip maker Conexant to supply chips to its broadband communication division. Conexant now competes directly with the mobile phone maker's current supplier, Broadcom Corp. Under the deal, Conexant will supply packages of chipsets and software to Motorola, primarily for use in set top boxes, cable modems, and voice-over internet protocol. The director of procurement at Motorola was quoted, "The infusion of competition will make an already good supplier (Broadcom) even better. It may be a negative for Broadcom because now they have true competition in the broadband space. But I think it's a net positive because it will help keep them very focused on our business and probably accelerate their product development in the market as well."[5]

The downside of dual sourcing is that it may force customers to double their supplier-specific investment. Relationships between employees from both sides must be established, IT systems adapted, and so forth. This additional investment may be justified if it is small relative to the higher risk of single sourcing.

Risk reduction requires dual sourcing to be volume-based rather than product-based. A product-based dual sourcing strategy defines a primary source responsible for unpredictable (or small batch) supplies and a secondary source responsible for predictable (or large batch) supplies. This involves *different* types of products. Lock-in to both sources results. A volume-based strategy sources the same product from two sources. With that, the primary site covers everyday demand whereas the secondary site is only used when demand fluctuates highly.

REDUCING BRAND-SPECIFIC INVESTMENT

Rational customers will try to reduce brand-specific investment even if insurance is available. Insurance is costly and cannot cover all risks resulting from lock-in. This raises the issue regarding what customers can do to reduce their lock-in.

Brand Choice

An easy way for customers to reduce lock-in is to choose a less entrenching brand that requires less specific investment. When is such a brand available?

Remember our discussion of the economics of markets with switching costs. Established vendors with a high market share find it more profitable to keep prices high for their locked-in customers and are less interested in enlarging their customer base by cutting prices or reducing lock-in. In contrast, in order to build a customer base, smaller or new players will develop alternative solutions that are either cheaper, less entrenching, or both.

Brands resulting in less lock-in are likely to emerge in markets with low barriers of entry. Lower barriers of entry lead to smaller

---

5 Source: http://www.valpeyfisher.com/doc/SupplyToMotorola.htm.

players entering the market, which is a good reason for offering less lock-in. It is their only chance against the Microsofts and SAPs of this world.

A good reason for established players to reduce lock-in is the market size effect. If strong lock-in deters the majority of potential buyers from becoming adopters, lock-in reduction will greatly enlarge the market and, in consequence, the customer base. This is the tradeoff between being a monopolist in a small market or being a contender in a large market. Because it is hard to estimate the market size effect, established companies find it less risky to keep discriminating against their customer base and not attracting new adopters. In fact, it can be better to let potential buyers wait forever for less entrenching brands.

For the customer, a less entrenching brand might mean to choose the second-best option. Logic requires buyers to choose highly idiosyncratic brands only if these offer more value and additional productivity. Then, first-best option is the brand with strong lock-in but with no risk of being exploited. As a supplier, you can use this motivation by not reducing lock-in but providing insurance for those who would otherwise prefer not to buy.

Performance-based Compensation

The sum of all brand- or vendor-specific investments results from many factors, including the training needed to become familiar with the technology, establishing good working relationships, and the price that the vendor charges. As a supplier, you can reduce the customer's perceived risk resulting from lock-in by changing your pricing concept and letting customers rent your product or service. What we mean by "price" is usually a lump sum. It is a certain amount of money that buyers pay up front or agree to pay later. Rarely is the price actually paid in any way related to the benefits the customer receives from consumption after the purchase. In many industries, a lump-sum charge is a sound model. Customers' perception of benefits from consumption will vary significantly among them and change over time. Customers may act opportunistically and state lower benefits than actually received in order to reduce costs. This would make for a risky revenue stream for the vendor. This lets companies prefer a constant price that is charged up front.

The opposite approach is the performance-based compensation model. In this model, the customers pay as they go. If they don't use the product or service, they don't pay anything. If they use it more, they pay more. It is very critical to exactly define performance. There should be no doubt between the vendor and customer what the criteria are by which performance is measured and how it is measured. An objective yardstick is absolutely necessary.

Note that Microsoft's "software assurance" package under the new pricing model is *not* a performance-based rent. It just spreads the price of a new license over several years. There is no connection to performance whatsoever.

In practice, a performance-based compensation is rarely found.[6] It seems that most companies find it too risky. However, it is a viable option. To some extent, it shifts the performance risk back to the vendor who may be able to handle it better. It is manageable if you find a performance measurement approach that is objective and fair.

SUMMARY

Lock-in resulting from brand-specific investment puts customers at risk. They may or may not be exploited by their suppliers after lock-in. Rational customers will anticipate their risk position after their entrenchment to a certain brand. Therefore, a company should assume that customers try to avoid lock-in traps.

Theoretically, customers can reduce the amount of brand-specific investment and insure the risk that remains. From the vendor's perspective, customers should not be motivated to choose less entrenching brands. Switching costs are a profit driver. Instead, vendors should opt for a differentiated set of insurance packages that attracts buyers with various risk preferences.

Vendors should be prepared to openly discuss with customers the degree of entrenchment that results from adopting their brand. Don't let customers run into traps. They will eventually find out and be dissatisfied, and that may hurt in the long run much more than any price discrimination can compensate.

---

6 IBM offers such a pricing model for blade centers. You pay depending on the performance you need. See http://www-1.ibm.com/servers/eserver/bladecenter/scod /more_info.html.

6

The New Approach to Market Segmentation

In markets with switching costs, a generic market segmentation approach fails. A different concept is required. Here's why.

In principle, market segmentation is the process of subdividing a market (all potential and actual buyers of a certain type of product or service) into distinct subsets. It is called *market* segmentation, but we are talking about the segmentation of potential *buyers*, not vendors.[1] Within those subsets or segments, customer needs and purchasing behavior are similar. Between the segments, they should be as different as possible.

Segmentation enables companies to differentiate marketing in order to address the different needs of different segments. It is the basis for product and service differentiation with customers self-selecting among the various offers. Because differentiation increases profits, the idea of market segmentation is appealing.

Advanced segmentation models employ a mixture of variables —socio-demographical (age, income, family size, and so on), psychological (lifestyle, values), and behavioral (usage levels, brand loyalty)—to identify market segments. In the car industry, for example, segmentation models are based on a combination of demographical variables usage criteria (for example, commuting habits) and psychological variables such as brand image and self-image. In the electric utility industry, segmentation is much simpler and centers around customer types (industrial, commercial, or residential) that accurately describe their usage behavior.

Different industries require different segmentation variables, because usage behavior and preferences are driven by different factors. In every industry, segmentation variables are supposed to capture the drivers of customer preference and product use. They

---

1 The concept of strategic groups is concerned with finding subsets of companies or business units with homogeneous strategies.

are employed to explain customers' purchasing behavior and should explain *why* customers buy the brands they buy.

Switching costs dramatically change the environment in an industry. With switching costs, customer preference loses its importance as a driver of purchasing behavior. Instead, brand choice in the past becomes a much more significant influence on future buying. Consequently, segmentation models which do not take customer lock-in into account are useless. Use a novel two-step approach for market segmentation in markets with switching costs:

1. Analyze the market structure on the basis of dynamic lock-in. Who is locked-in in relation to repurchasing cycles? This segmentation is based on customer accessibility.
2. Analyze locked-in customers with regard to the origin and extent of their switching costs, to establish the propensity of customers to switch.

STEP ONE: SEGMENTING THE MARKET

In each market with switching costs, there are three segments (see Figure 6-1).

- new buyers ("first-timers")
- users with or without irrelevant switching costs
- entrenched users who have significant switching costs because of previous brand choice

New buyers have not made any binding purchase decisions in the past. When they choose a certain brand or supplier, they are "first-timers" and are switching cost-free. A good example is photographers who love analog technology and are still thinking about "going digital." Since adoption of a new technology is never complete (meaning that every potential buyer has made at least one purchase decision), there are always first-timers in the market—even in mature industries. Their number typically declines over time.[2]

---

2 As with every new technology, there are always some diehards who are proud not to adopt new technology. Take APUG.ORG for example. They describe themselves as an "online community of like-minded individuals devoted to traditional (non-digital) photographic processes" (see www. apug.org). Even today, there are music lovers who would only consider turn-table record players and wouldn't go near a CD player. New product adoption is never complete throughout the market.

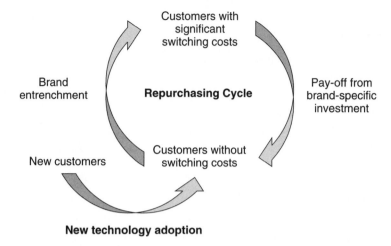

Figure 6-1: Market Segmentation Model with Switching Costs (First Step)

The second segment is the locked-in users that have bought a certain brand recently. Because of their brand-specific investment, the members of this segment have switching costs and are locked-in. With this segment, it is important to look at the extent and origin of their switching costs.

The third segment consists of users with little or no switching costs who have made a purchase in the past, but this purchase no longer binds them in their perception. This may be because they feel that the old investment has paid off and it is time to "move on." Or they may think that an alternative brand or technology offers more value which justifies switching. In any case, members of the third segment are ready to switch.

Note the crucial difference between "new buyers" and "users without switching costs." Users without switching costs have brand experience and have made purchase decisions in the past that will probably influence their purchase decisions in the future. They may consciously switch brands (from A to B) in order to eliminate their reverse switching costs (back to A), and increase their future flexibility in brand choice. New buyers have no relevant brand experience, whatsoever. They may or may not intend to make brand-specific investments that will result in lock-in.

Every user runs through a repurchasing cycle that starts with brand choice, and then runs through a process of increasing brand-entrenchment. Switching costs increase. Think of an eBay customer who becomes more savvy over time with designing successful eBay auctions. The repurchasing cycle starts when customers, who believed they had accumulated all possible benefits from a brand-specific investment, buy more.

This segmentation concept addresses a number of important questions.

1. How many new buyers are still "up for grabs?" The size of this segment is one of the most important drivers of price competition. The more new buyers are in the marketsIn the fiercer price competition will be.
2. How many customers are in the market with significant switching costs? This segment is more or less untouchable by new entries or smaller players. In effect, it is "out-of-market."
3. What is the length of the repurchasing cycle? When can customers be expected to seriously consider changing their principle supplier or brand? This length effectively drives market size. The longer the repurchasing cycle, the lower is the number of experienced buyers "in the market."

If you are a new entry or a smaller player, don't aim too high. Companies can expect to compete for new buyers and those users whose repurchasing cycle is about to start anew. If the repurchase cycle is long (consider office software or expensive porcelain where the repurchase cycle can be as long as 10 years), this reduces the yearly potential of buyers who can be expected to change brands. The target market is that beyond which a customer base shrinks with a longer repurchase cycle.

Note that this is a dynamic model. Lock-in is temporary and ends when customers decide to abandon technology or knowledge that binds them when purchasing complements, updates, or spare parts. Lock-in also ends when airline customers have used up all their bonus miles and are "back to zero." Technological innovation affects the perceived value of brand-specific investment. The introduction of jet engines for commercial aircraft in the 1950s drastically devalued airlines' experience with piston engine aircraft. The advantages of jet air travel were far greater than the disadvantage of writing off the intimate knowledge with old technology. Similarly, the development of high-resolution digital photography devalues brand-specific investment into analog photography. Technological innovation can motivate customers to abandon old technologies in favor of new solutions even if switching costs are high. Many factors influence the evolution of lock-in.

In markets with switching costs, companies need to think about accessibility of customers as well as their preferences. Accessibility is determined by the customer's perceived value of brand-specific investment. A customer who values brand-specific investment very highly will be locked-in for the foreseeable future. A good example is an Excel user who has invested heavily into brand-specific learning (for example, training with macro-programming) and believes this knowledge is very useful and up-to-date. This user is virtually inaccessible for any supplier other than Microsoft. In contrast, a customer who thinks brand-specific investment has lost its value is highly accessible for other suppliers.

STEP TWO: SEGMENTING LOCKED-IN CUSTOMERS

Next, we analyze locked-in customers. Locked-in customers can present a significant proportion of a company's market as seen in the market for operating systems or the ERP software industry. The segment of locked-in customers is usually very heterogeneous which means it will not respond uniformly to marketing efforts. This requires further segmentation with regard to the origin and extent of their lock-in. Analyze the segment of locked-in customers in the following stages.

1. Analyze the actual purchasing and usage behavior to establish the users' ability to switch in the foreseeable future. The ability to switch determines the accessibility of potential, but locked-in customers. The nature and degree of lock-in can be very different.
2. Determine the preferences of users independent from switching cost influences. Which brand do they prefer? What are the preference drivers?
3. Find out what the users' risk-taking behavior is. Are they risk averse or risk prone? The more risk averse they are, the less likely is a switch.
4. Question 1 addresses customers' ability to switch. But this is only one side of the equation. Customers must also *want* to switch. Therefore, questions 2 and 3 address potential buyers' propensity to switch. Accessible users are more likely to switch if they prefer other brands and accept the risk of switching.

Accessibility of Locked-in Customers

Here is a fictitious illustration of the approach for step 2 in market segmentation.

Recently, companies in the consumer packaged goods (CPG) industry with large field forces have tried to leverage their investment into enterprise resource planning software by extending information flows beyond the walls of the company and across the challenging "last mile" to sales reps in the field. The idea is to optimize field force performance through mobile information solutions (MIS).

The implementation of this idea requires a combination of task-specific software to enable the information flow, mobile communication devices that provide access to the database from wherever reps go and, of course, training of reps and software engineers.

Applications of this technology can be found in B2C where CPG makers use extensive sales forces to service retailers and their locations. Retailers demand more and more classic retail functions to be performed by CPG makers, fueling the need to empower field personnel.

The CPG industry is huge and diverse. Players such as Coca-Cola or Procter & Gamble use extensive sales forces to service a multitude of retail locations. Of those, about 90% have implemented some sort of MIS for their field forces. The rest are reluctant to adopt because the advantages are small with smaller companies. The real power of MIS for field forces comes with a strong ERP backbone and the need to coordinate large field forces—both issues favor larger companies as clients.

Total investment for MIS can be in the area of $3,000–$5,000 per sales rep including training costs (which account for roughly half of that). More than 80% of the total investment can be brand-specific, because the software, its interface to the portable device, and the ERP systems are proprietary. However, the share of brand-specific investment varies among products.

A number of MIS software suppliers are specialized in offering turn-key solutions. Together, five suppliers hold more than 80% of the market. The rest belong to a large number of smaller players who are not supposed to survive the shakeout that is to be expected. The three largest players (A, B, C) are established companies who have been instrumental in establishing MIS as a recognized tool in the CPG industry. The two smaller companies (D, E) are more recent entries. D entered only 5 years ago, E shortly before that.

Compared to other failed start-ups, D and E have been hugely successful despite their late entry. Their success is due to a sharp focus on neglected market niches. On that basis, they developed sound technology and business models and have started to expand beyond their niches. In both cases, this move is very promising.

The most important determinant of segment membership among locked-in customers is brand ownership. Since this is an industry with high brand-specific investment and high switching costs, it is extremely probable that customers are very brand-loyal when purchasing complements or updates for MIS.

Brand ownership is given by each brand's share of installed customer base. This is the percentage of each brand with regard to the total number of users. Note that market share is defined differently: sales divided by total sales *per year*. With switching costs, customers who bought two or three years ago can still be effectively locked-in. Take this into account by extending the time horizon.

With each brand in the market, the degree of brand-specific investment (brand-specific investment divided by total investment) can vary and it often does. Different brands may require more training and adaptation than others. It is important to establish the degree to which a brand requires specific investment. Assume that this degree is about the same for all customers because it is more brand-driven and less customer-driven.

Differentiate between three levels of brand-specific investment: very high, high, and moderate. To find the appropriate levels depends on your industry. In the ERP software business, 60%–70% of the total investment in customer projects is not IT hardware-related. IT hardware is pretty much generic. ERP software is not. However, brand-specific investment cannot exceed the value of non-standardized elements of some type of product (here: 70%). Thus, 40%–50% could be considered as a moderate degree of brand-specific investment, 50%–60% as high and 60–70% as very high. It is obvious that higher shares of brand-specific investment add to customer lock-in.

Next, you need to find out how far current users are in their repurchasing cycle. This requires you to get an idea of how long MIS for field forces are used and when customers are ready to reconsider their previous brand choice.

In our case, industry experts believe that users stick to a system for at least six to eight years in order to earn an adequate return on investment (ROI). Users may switch systems earlier if they are very unsatisfied with its performance, or may update a system more aggressively and thereby extend its life span. Six to eight years seems to be a good average. Experts also say that a technological breakthrough that dramatically increases user benefits may motivate users to abandon their system earlier. But they don't expect that over the next two to three years.

With an average MIS lifespan of seven years, it is critical to ascertain when current users have implemented their current system. A company needs to know when competitors A to E sold their MIS to their respective clients. A simplified approach would be to add seven years to the year in which the system was implemented, giving the average year of repurchase.

Together, the degree of brand-specific investment and the repurchase time determine the accessibility of locked-in customers. It is important to realize that the two variables can compensate each other. High specific investment becomes less important when customers are getting closer to repurchase. Figure 6-2 illustrates this relationship.

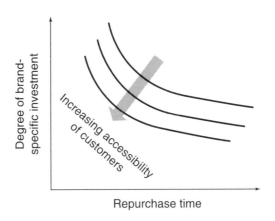

Figure 6-2: Accessibility of Locked-in Customers

The compensation effect between the two variables is illustrated by several indifference curves which each depict a given level of accessibility of locked-in customers. Lower levels of brand-specific investment and less time until repurchase increase customer accessibility. Again, it would be difficult to establish the exact mathematical relationship. But for practical purposes, a good estimate is often sufficient. Remember, we only need to establish customer accessibility on an ordinal level (high versus low) Table 6-1 on page 66 summarizes this information for the MIS case and provides an estimate of customer accessibility. It shows the installed base for each brand, the degree of brand-specific investment, and the average time until repurchase.

In the MIS case, customers of supplier A are moderately accessible although many have implemented their current system five years ago. This is due to the fact that this is the system with the highest level of specificity.

> When company A moved into the market as a pioneer, it quickly sold its very idiosyncratic but powerful solution to first-time customers and set an early market standard. With the entry of several other potent suppliers, it lost significant market share (specifically to B and C) and now makes more than 70% of its profits with updates and cross-selling to its customer base. Marketing and product development of supplier A is primarily targeted at motivating users to update instead of acquiring new customers.

In comparison, users of company C are highly accessible. They use the system with the lowest degree of specificity, meaning they can transfer more of their expertise with MIS to other systems.

> Company C entered the MIS market with the claim that training of sales reps would be minimal as they used as many Microsoft tools in its software as possible. This led to very short implementation processes, effectively cutting training costs by 60%. C also adapted its solution to the ERP system of the market leader as much as possible and reduced software implementation costs significantly. This resulted in cost savings of 40%–50% for the client.

> At the same time, clients had to accept that the "C solution" provided only the very indispensable features for mobile field forces. Many "nice to have" features that A or B offered were not available with C. But this appealed to many first-time buyers and led to a significant increase of the total market. Today, industry observers say that C was instrumental in expanding the market beyond the likes of Pepsi-Cola or Kellogg.

Customers of company D are "out of bounds." Their system is highly binding and in many cases very young. The situation with users of B and E is similar, although less extreme.

Table 6-1: Customer Accessibility Assessment for MIS Case

SUPPLIER	A	B	C	D	E
Share of installed base	28%	21%	19%	8%	6%
Brand-specific investment	↑ (very high)	↗ (high)	→ (moderate)	↗ (high)	→ (moderate)
Average repurchase (years)	1.5	2.5	2	4	3.5
Accessibility (within 1–2 years)	Moderate	Low	High	Very Low	Low
Attractiveness of segment	+	−	++	− −	−

Segments of locked-in users become more attractive with larger size (installed base) and higher accessibility. In Table 6-1, attractiveness of segments is indicated on a scale ranging from ++ to − −. This analysis shows that A-users and C-users are the most attractive segments. Both are large segments with many users moving into the stage of reconsidering their brand choice.

Propensity to Switch

Customers switch if they can and want to. Whether they *want* to switch is a question of preference and attitude towards risk.

PREFERENCE ANALYSIS Preferences indicate which alternative a buyer chooses over another. If you prefer a Lexus over a BMW (all other things being equal), then you have a preference for a Lexus car over a BMW. Besides budget constraints, preferences are the most important drivers of buying behavior of consumers and organizations.

In most applications of preference analysis, so-called "multi-criterion models" are used. We like to think (and there is a lot of reasons to do so) that preferences are the result of a customer's evaluation of multiple criteria for alternative offers. Cars, for example, are typically evaluated on a number of criteria such as brand image, price, and quality—among others. Customers evaluate the brands or models they consider on the basis of these criteria to find the best mix. This is a typical application for a multi-criterion preference model. Academic research has analyzed this problem extensively and has developed a number of statistical methods to find out what criteria are important to customers and how important they are. A typical empirical preference study combines conjoint analysis and cluster analysis to identify groups of customers with distinctive preference structures. Both methods are standard elements of market research studies.

Multi-criterion models apply to rational buying decisions that are primarily information-driven. Brand choice can also be habitual or driven by emotional impulse and require different approaches to brand choice analysis.

What companies need to do is the following.

1. Find out which criteria are relevant to potential buyers when evaluating the different brands and find out how important the different criteria are to them. Importance can vary substantially between individual customers.
2. Find out how potential buyers evaluate brands using these criteria.

With this information in your hands, you should be able to explain fairly well why buyers buy the brands they buy given that no constraints keep them from buying the most preferred alternative.

The selection and implementation of MIS for field forces is a complex task that probably involves several departments of a company. Sales, IT, and organization will all want to have a say in the decision. Board members will focus of the impact of MIS on the overall profitability of the company, whereas departments will look at MIS from their specific perspective. Therefore, we will observe a broad mix of criteria such as the following.

- ability to improve service quality and sales functions
- ability to develop valuable new sales functions
- resulting overall cost reduction (sales, outbound logistics)
- ease of implementation (time, costs)
- adaptability to ERP system and organizational processes
- life cycle costs including investment in new IT hardware
- (ongoing) support from supplier, references

Such a list helps explain what brands buyers are going to choose. It is the basis on which to estimate the propensity to switch brands. Customers who believe other brands offer higher benefits are more likely to switch. When conducting such an analysis, keep in mind that all that counts is customer perception. There is no such thing as objectivity in brand performance. It is very important not let personal perceptions (especially of competitive offers) be blinding. Have you ever heard a salesperson say that his offer is not the best? Conduct market research and ask potential buyers. Accept the results, even if they are not desirable. Remember, customers buy, not companies.

RISK PREFERENCE As users of a certain brand, locked-in customers can evaluate this brand very well. Other brands are harder to evaluate because of the lack of first-hand experience. This makes brand switching a risky endeavor as the advantages of the brand they switch to are uncertain.

Risk refers to the probability of an unwanted event occurring and the severity of potential loss. Risk increases when the probability of a loss and/or its severity increases. This leads to the conclusion that buyers' risk preference will influence their propensity to switch brands. In general, the more users are ready to accept risk ("risk-taking"), the more probable is a brand switch.

> Often we find indicators for buyers' attitude towards risk in their purchasing history. In the MIS case, C users were attracted by the limited amount of its brand specificity. They seem to be more risk-averse than adopters of B, who accepted higher risk even when a low risk option (C) was present. Early adopters of the pioneer brand A showed a significant degree of risk-taking. Considering that D and E developed out of small market niches, we might conclude that their customers found that the higher risk of unproven innovations were outweighed by better adaptation to their needs.

The role of risk in consumer and industrial buying has been researched extensively. One important finding is that in practice buyers engage in risk-reducing activities. This includes an extensive information search and sticking to "well proven" sources of supply. However, the following issues might motivate a buyer to accept more risk than usual.

- outside pressure from important customers or suppliers, leaving no choice but to engage in a risky purchasing decision
- the "bandwagon effect," a widely held belief in industry that a certain strategy is indispensable for success
- a favorable financial situation which reduces the perceived severity of loss

These issues are just examples of factors that moderate buyers' attitude towards risk in specific situations.

When measuring attitude towards risk in a brand choice situation, we do not have such sophisticated and well-tested methods at our disposal as with preference analysis. Because of this, companies should allow for some degree of error. You can target a user segment where you feel that buyers are highly risk-averse when you can offer overwhelming and proven performance advantages.

PROPENSITY TO SWITCH   Propensity to switch is determined by perceived relative brand performance ("a Lexus is better than a BMW") and perceived risk of switching. To some degree, the two variables can compensate each other. The same propensity to switch is achieved with high performance advantage/high risk or small performance advantage/small risk.

Figure 6-3 illustrates an example. Let's say a company wants to establish the trade-off between performance and risk for a 70% probability to switch brands. Performance must increase in order to compensate for increasing risk. This means that in order to motivate a risk-averse buyer to switch, you need more performance advantage than for a risk-taker. In the example depicted in Figure 6-3, performance advantage increases exponentially indicated by the decreasing slope of the curve. It follows that it becomes more and more difficult to attract buyers from segments of locked-in users when they perceive higher risk. Eventually, the cost of increasing performance to compensate for risk will be prohibitive. This is the point where the supplier's expected return from brand switch becomes negative.

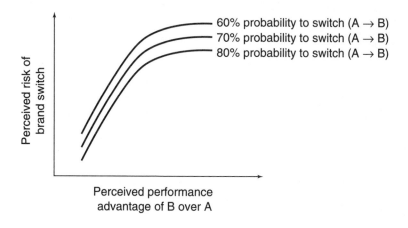

Figure 6-3: Propensity to Switch

PUTTING IT ALL TOGETHER:
A NEW SEGMENTATION MODEL

The last step is to integrate information on segment accessibility and propensity to switch in a systematic fashion. For the MIS case, the result is given in Table 6-2.

For the MIS case, extensive market research across all user segments was conducted to supply the relevant information. The following results were obtained:

A users are a very diverse group with heterogeneous preferences. This is because supplier A was the first to offer a comprehensive MIS solution and therefore attracted a wide range of customer types who are now locked-in. A has updated its system regularly. The perceived performance advantage is small to medium. Only solution D is perceived to be a viable alternative.

Users of D and E are very loyal to their suppliers not only because of switching costs, but also because of their system's near perfect fit to their needs. Consequently, these customers are not inclined to switch.

The propensity of B users to switch is significant. They are highly attracted by the low level of brand-specific investment required by solution C. This could result in much lower MIS life cycle costs (training, updates, etc.). Also, some larger companies in that group like the idea of increasing their strategic flexibility by switching. A switch back to B would be easy because of the brand-specific knowledge in the company.

Table 6-2: Segmentation Model Based on MIS Case

USERS	A	B	C	D	E
Accessibility (within 1–2 years)	Moderate	Low	High	Very low	Low
Attitude towards risk	High risk takers	Taker	Averse	Taker	Neutral
Performance advantage (as a result of switching)	Small to medium (to D)	Large (to C)	Medium (to E)	Very small	Very small
Propensity to switch	+	++	+	– –	– –
Comment	Diverse group, heterogeneous preferences	Highly attracted by low brand-specific investment in C, strategic flexibility (back to B)	Provider of E adapts solution specifically to C users	See no advantage in abandoning "tailor-made" system	Ditto

Again, this model is not supposed to provide an accurate estimate of customers' probability to switch brands. The probability to switch is determined by many factors. Accessibility of customers and their propensity to switch are the key variables in the segmentation of locked-in customers. In your market analysis, you should focus on them.

SUMMARY OF PART 2

Switching costs are important drivers of customer equity. In a perfect market without any sustainable competitive advantage, the value of your customer base exactly equals their collective switching costs. The higher switching costs are, the more your business is worth—and vice versa. Switching costs offer a source of profitable price discrimination which can survive even fierce competition. A case in point is commercial aviation. A closer analysis of pricing in this highly competitive industry shows that bonus miles programs are largely used to implement effective price discrimination against locked-in customers. This is why, in markets with switching costs, market share is a key driver of future profits.

Rivalry in an industry is reduced as a result of switching costs. This shields incumbents against new entries and the resulting erosion of profits. It also shields them against market share battles within the industry. Complements and merging technologies that serve as complements play an important part in creating switching costs and must be considered a crucial element of industry analysis.

Switching costs result in significant changes to buying behavior and lead to a new approach in market segmentation. Rational customers try to avoid lock-in traps. They may reduce the amount of brand-specific investment or look for insurance or both. Suppliers should adopt a proactive stance by offering insurance through contract and reputation.

Market segmentation should focus on the accessibility of potential customers and their propensity to switch. Brand preference loses its importance as a driver of buying behavior and must be analyzed in context with buyers' risk preference.

PART 3

Creating Switching Costs: Instruments for Robust Customer Loyalty

Customer lock-in is about creating switching costs. Switching costs increase customer loyalty and the vendor's share-of-wallet. In this chapter, we will look at the different instruments for creating switching costs, focusing on how these instruments work and under what circumstances they are appropriate.

Don't confuse switching costs and brand loyalty. Higher switching costs will automatically lead to higher loyalty, but the reverse is not necessarily true: high loyalty doesn't mean that switching costs exist. Customers can be very brand loyal without having any measurable switching costs.

With switching costs, customer loyalty becomes robust. It is not affected by short-term changes of a brand's relative quality or pricing because customers are locked-in. Even if an alternative is better, customers stay for as long as switching costs are sufficiently high.

In many industries, brand loyalty is not robust because there are no (or marginal) switching costs. Think of breakfast cereals or TV news channels. You may have developed a preference for one, but this will only hold until there is a better one or you have changed your mind. This is called precarious brand loyalty because it is vulnerable. Customers can switch anytime, and many do.

Companies try to counter this problem by differentiating their products and services. Product differentiation refers to a product feature (a "unique selling preposition") that other companies do not offer. In many cases, product differentiation fails to create robust customer loyalty.

Product differentiation refers to what the company does. When American Airlines introduces more legroom to the coach class, it differentiates its service from competitors. Any competitor can duplicate that and the faster they do, the more vulnerable this strategy is.

On the other hand, switching costs refer to what the customer has to do or learn. If that is vendor- or brand-specific, then a potential for switching costs arises. This creates robust customer loyalty.

Another problem with product differentiation is that it is ineffective in markets where variety-seeking is rampant. Variety-seeking refers to the consumer's tendency to switch brands to experience "something new." Brand change itself provides a benefit to customers. In markets for hedonic products such as bars, restaurants, music, or leisure activities, variety-seeking is common.

In markets with intensive variety-seeking, you either offer a constant stream of new products and features or your customers switch for the sake of switching. Static product differentiation fails to create customer loyalty.

So what can companies do instead? The following chapters discuss the different strategies to create loyalty based on switching costs.

7

Motivate and Enable Brand-specific Learning

Brand-specific learning is an essential driver of switching costs. The interesting question is how companies can create learning-based lock-in. The case of Sun Star Office demonstrates the importance of customer learning. Because users of Microsoft Office have learned so much about this software, they are very reluctant to switch to different software, even if this software is free. Learning costs can be a very powerful force to create switching costs. Look at other industries to see how learning works.

CASE: EBAY

Second to none among auction houses, eBay is one of the few dot-coms that is making money—and it has been doing so nearly from inception. Its growth rate and market capitalization are outstanding. eBay started as an exchange for Pez dispensers and has grown into an auction powerhouse. Today, 20% of all person-to-person package shipments in the U.S. are the result of eBay auctions.

Auctions are very effective in extracting willingness-to-pay from buyers. This has led Sotheby's former CEO to estimate that prices for collectibles under $10,000 will rise by more than 10% due to the sharply increasing number of on-line buyers who wouldn't have considered an off-line auction.

eBay has been very successful in creating customer switching costs on the basis of learning. eBay sellers acquire learning costs in two ways.

- Over time, eBay sellers establish a historical record of their auctions. Buyers can evaluate the seller's performance and post detailed comments of the seller's behavior. On that basis, sellers establish a reputation. Since potential buyers neither touch nor feel what they are about to buy and cannot meet the seller in person, reputation becomes a safeguard against opportunistic behavior on the seller's part. This historical record is lost when sellers switch to another auction house.

- Optimization of eBay auctions requires specific knowledge about auction implementation at eBay, especially for professional auction or "powersellers" who complete hundreds of auctions per week. eBay offers automated data exchange and other features targeted at professional users. To learn this takes time, which leads to such costs.

A seller's reputation at eBay is valuable because it drives the final auction price. Daniel Houser and John Wooders from the University of Arizona looked into the relationship between reputation and auction price at eBay. They found that more positive comments about a seller resulted in a higher auction price for the same item.[1] This shows that a seller's historical record is valuable and presents significant switching costs. It cannot be transferred to another auction house.

Also, the knowledge that eBay sellers acquire is to a certain extent idiosyncratic: it is *eBay-specific*. It takes re-learning to sell with the same success and speed at other auction houses and to build the same reputation.

The eBay case demonstrates that to create learning-based switching costs, two things have to happen.

1. Companies must motivate customers to learn. This motivation is strong if learning is necessary to use a product or service properly. Its value to the customer must increase the more knowledge she has about how it works and the benefits it provides. A good condition for that is when products are used over an extended period of time. Because the auction price is directly linked to a seller's reputation and to his level of expertise with eBay's auction tools, this motivation is strong for eBay users.

2. Companies must *enable* learning. Learning is enabled if a product is *idiosyncratic*, for example, if it is different from others. Customers must adapt to the product, not vice versa. However, idiosyncrasy is only a necessary condition. Companies must also *facilitate* learning by offering a learning environment. Look up eBay's website and you find an integrated system of written information and video-based instruction on

---

1 See: D. Houser and J. Wooders: Reputation in Auctions: Theory and Evidence from EBay, Working Paper, Department of Economics, University of Arizona, October 2001, source: http://bpaosf.bpa.arizona.edu/~jwooders/revision.pdf.

how to sell by auction. Companies can also attend one-day seminars all over the U.S. in which trainers demonstrate simple, but also more sophisticated tools in designing an auction. eBay tries to keep the barrier to customer learning low.

The intriguing element about learning at eBay is the step-by-step learning approach, which creates gradual customer lock-in. To learn how to run a simple auction is not very difficult. The entry barrier is low. Sellers are motivated to learn more and become more adept. They realize that more knowledge leads to better auctions and higher earnings potential.

The bottom line is that eBay motivates and facilitates learning at the same time. It is very efficient in developing superior, but at the same time eBay-specific, solutions to on-line auctions. eBay's idiosyncratic and rich in customer learning auction model differs substantially from that of competitors.

CASE: SPORTS WEBSITES

Albeit to a lesser extent, the same principle applies to sports websites.[2]

> Mark Mathias, president of the ebusiness information consulting firm Eureka Digital, is quoted as saying: "Let's say that I have a sports website and I find that a particular visitor always looks at the hockey scores through three or four clicks. If I can now recognize that Joe Hockey Fan likes hockey scores, why shouldn't I, the website, automatically put the hockey scores on the home page that I deliver to the hockey fan?
>
> "What that does is make the hockey fan more attuned to my website because we have met that customer's needs. We've said, 'We can detect that you're interested in hockey scores because every time you visit us, you go look at the hockey scores.' That may change from season to season, but the point is that's how people think. That's how they like to get their information, and even more importantly, you're developing a relationship. You are creating switching costs."

This is a case in which a user's click stream is used to customize a service. Changing the website means that the same cus-

2 This excerpt was taken from http://www.okec.org/news/1to1.htm.

tomer has to go through the same process to trigger the same customization. This can be a significant barrier to switching. Amazon.com did the same with its one-click purchasing function.

CASE: BMW

Product idiosyncrasies and product differentiation are not the same. Product differentiation refers to any feature of a product that is different from competitive offerings. Audi and Cadillac have different climate control systems for their luxury sedans, and their cars also look and feel different. Both car makers, however, try to make their cars self-explanatory, almost eliminating the need for brand-specific learning. Even without reading the manual, you can certainly drive both—or any other car, as a matter of fact.

Why does the car industry fail to establish learning-based switching costs? Car manufacturers invest a lot of money into research and development to create brand-specific product features and a distinctive brand image. On the other hand, the car industry is a mature industry. Mature industries develop standards. Competitors are highly motivated to follow standards to achieve cost savings. This makes the implementation of idiosyncrasies difficult.

Customers in the car industry expect a minimum of brand-specific learning. It seems to be an unwritten rule of the industry not to make customers really "learn" their car. The use of some functions (navigation, climate control, or audio system) may require some learning, but this does little to create substantial learning-based switching costs.

> Every rule has an exception. Swedish car maker Saab has been famous for pieces of idiosyncratic engineering. Saab engineers insisted on placing the ignition key on the center console. Pulling the key was only possible in reverse gear which then engages a lock that blocks the transmission. This was an anti-theft device much more effective than a regular steering column lock. Today, significant learning and switching costs arise with the diffusion of complex software in cars. BMW has been hit over its head with criticism of iDrive, a novel one-stick control system for the 7-series that controls several hundred functions. It seems to be so complicated, auto website www.pistonheads.com comments: "Like the customers who will eventually use it, iDrive will either adapt or die."[3]

---

3 See: http://www. pistonheads.com/truth/default.asp?storyId=6008.

Despite the criticism voiced over the complexity of BMW's iDrive control system, it actually *is* an attempt at triggering brand-specific learning. It actually does take an hour or two to learn how iDrive works. This is somewhat unusual in this industry and it is an indicator that BMW is willing to take a risk. It is too early to determine the influence of iDrive on BMW brand loyalty. The idea is that once users have adapted to iDrive and learned how to use it, they will try to economize on that brand-specific investment by being more loyal to BMW.[4] The eloquent experts at www.pistonheads.com may miss the point: we should look at iDrive not only as a tool supposed to facilitate the use of a modern car brimming with electronics, but also as an instrument to create learning costs based on product idiosyncrasy.

THE ESSENCE OF CUSTOMER LEARNING

Only product idiosyncrasies provide potential for customer learning. Idiosyncratic product features make it necessary for customers to adapt. This is to some extent contrary to marketing philosophy that calls for giving the customer what they want. Brand-specific learning is typically not what the customer wants. The reason is that it is costly and creates learning-based switching costs. The result is brand dependency. Customer learning must involve a trade-off: learning is the price customers pay for higher value. Only more value motivates customers to invest in brand-specific knowledge.

To facilitate learning, companies must lower entry barriers to brand-specific information and instruction. A good way to do that is a gradual learning process. This process leads customers through the learning process step-by-step and results in gradual lock-in. It is a piecemeal approach to customer learning in which success on each step motivates customers to keep going.

In an industry with standardized products, the potential for learning-based switching costs is small. Products are technologically exchangeable and customers have a lot of know-how. Firms may have to introduce new and radical technology to start the process of customer learning.

---

4 With the introduction of the new 5-series in summer of 2003, BMW has modified iDrive. BMW claims that it is now simpler and easier to use. Some functions—such as climate controls—now have separate controls as before. This indicates that BMW believes learning costs to be less important than ease-of-use. Their belief in idiosyncrasy only goes so far.

8

Understand and Seek Contractual Lock-in

Contractual customer lock-in occurs when vendors and customers agree on a contract that limits the customers' future flexibility in sourcing. It is not sufficient that customers indicate their preference to buy from a certain vendor. They must be limited in their future purchasing options—preferably to a single vendor or service provider. Customers don't like limited flexibility. From their perspective, it is better to keep as many options open as possible, because the future is uncertain.

Why, then, should customers agree to some form of contractual lock-in? In economics, the answer is always the same: They do, if contractual lock-in involves a trade-off that tips the scale in favor of a long-term, flexibility limiting sourcing arrangement. Or in simpler words: They do, if customers get something in return for limited flexibility that is more beneficial than being locked-in for some time. This again shines the light on the question, what do customers get for being locked-in.

CONTRACTUAL LOCK-IN IN B2B

In the business-to-business arena, contractual lock-in accompanies partner-specific investment that can only pay off over time. Partner-specific investment comes in very different shapes and sizes.

- Vertical R&D cooperation in which suppliers develop new technology for a customer or specific components of a customer's new product.
- Supplier-manufacturer coordination, in which parties engage in supply-chain management activities.
- Fixed-term contracts and evergreen contracts that minimize search costs.

Vertical R&D Cooperation

R&D cooperation with suppliers is common in the car industry and the hearing aid instrument industry. New technology for specific product components is jointly developed with suppliers who then become exclusive suppliers of these components.

> The hearing aid industry presents an interesting case of customer lock-in through contractual based R&D cooperation. According to an industry survey by Kristina Lee and Peter Lotz of Copenhagen Business School, about 5 million hearing instruments are sold per year worldwide at an average of $200 per unit.[1] In terms of market share changes and introduction of new technology, this industry is inert. Siemens from Germany is the largest player, followed by Starkey (U.S.) and Oticon (Denmark). The 10 largest manufacturers have a combined market share of more than 80%. Products fall into three categories: behind-the-ear (BTE), in-the-ear (ITE), and in-the-canal (ITC).

> With regard to the relationship between manufacturers and suppliers of hearing instrument components, the study concludes:[2]

> "Each component interacts with all other components in the small space available in the shell of a hearing instrument. . . . Once a component has been designed into a specific hearing instrument model, it typically will not be substituted by another supplier's components, neither a cheaper one nor a better one (since one better component can rarely improve the performance of a whole instrument), thus establishing switching costs. . . . These costs stem from required changes in testing, documentation, design, production processing, and purchasing. The industry, thus, estimates that the time it takes to switch from one electro-mechanical component to another is about two years."

Since hearing instrument manufacturers have decided to outsource the development and manufacturing of critical components such as transducers (microphones, receivers) and amplifiers, their dependence on suppliers such as Knowles or RTI has increased sharply.

---

1 Available at: http://www.cbs.dk/departments/ivs/wp/cis-nois.pdf.
2 See K. Lee and P. Lotz: Noise and Silence in the Hearing Instrument Industry, Working Paper, Copenhagen Business School, 1998.

The hearing aid case demonstrates that, from the supplier's perspective, the ability to create customer lock-in largely depends on its technological competence. If superior, OEMs can be motivated to suspend in-house development of critical components in spite of the resulting lock-in effect. Then, long-term contracts are in the OEM's interest to secure an important source of supply.

Supply-chain Management

In operation, coordination of supply chains with suppliers and customers can dramatically improve the efficiency in the supply chain. Take the case of the world's #1 retailer, Wal-Mart, which has to coordinate a rather complex structure of continuous flows of supplies to multiple Wal-Mart stores and Supercenters:

The cost efficiency of Wal-Mart's inventory management system as well as that of its suppliers depends on the integration of information systems (IOS). Integration rests upon point-of-sale data feeding coordinated inventory management processes in real time.

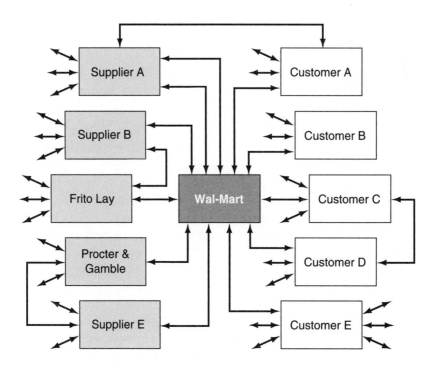

Figure 8-1: Wal-Mart's Supply Chain
(taken from http://www.ics.uci.edu/~wscacchi/Tech-EC/EC-B2B/B2B.ppt)

Despite all the good things about integration of information systems (reduced inventory and cycle time, faster transactions with less errors, etc.), the critical issue is compatibility and lock-in.

For example, Gillette is a supplier to both Wal-Mart and K-Mart. After having agreed on an IOS interface with Wal-Mart, Gilette found out that K-Mart wanted integration, too—only with a different interface. This problem of suppliers having to manage multiple and proprietary IOS interfaces is now more than 20 years old. And this has not changed since then, as Thomas Davenport of Accenture notes:[3]

> "Companies now prefer to have their ES communicate directly with each other using XML over the Internet, but they still must determine how to interface their information and business processes with their trading partners. They must ensure that both parties to a trade agree on what the term 'order quantity' and a vast number of other information entities mean . . . . Neither ERP nor XML nor the Internet has made such negotiations any easier. Even when two companies have the same enterprise system package, they may well have configured their information and processes very differently. Although some efforts are being made by firms like Vitria to solve these problems through the use of technology that intelligently 'interprets' what a particular definition or process means based on its context, these approaches are still under development and have not been widely adopted."

The result of this is clear. As long as the supplier-OEM/retailer interface is unique, implementing IOS creates significant switching costs. Wal-Mart simply cannot exchange one supplier for another even if their products are exchangeable. To some degree, Wal-Mart and K-Mart are locked-in to their suppliers.

The same principle applies to the car industry, in which manufacturers have not only outsourced the production of many components, but have forced suppliers to move production facilities close to the plants to facilitate JIT delivery and increase the efficiency (as in case of retailers) of inventory management.

Both R&D cooperation and IOS-based supply chain management are examples for extensive supplier-customer cooperation. Lock-in arises on both sides. Long-term contracts then serve as an instrument for customers to secure sources of supply.

---

3 Source: http://www.accenture.com/xdoc/en/ideas/isc/pdf/NGES_RN7_Connecting_Enterpris_Solutions.pdf.

Fixed-term Contracts and Evergreen Contracts

Long-term contracts reduce transaction costs and eliminate the need to constantly search and evaluate alternative suppliers. This search cost advantage comes at the price of reduced choice and lock-in.

A fixed-term contract ends after some time and may be renewed if the parties agree or may be renegotiated along the way. An evergreen contract renews itself automatically with no change in terms, if it is not terminated by the contracting parties. Typically, evergreen contracts regulate the advance notice time in which the contract can be terminated. Customer lock-in arises for the duration of the contract (fixed-term) or the advance notice time (evergreen).

Evergreen contracts can be instruments to achieve cost efficiency in sourcing, as the AMEC example demonstrates:

British engineering services giant AMEC (see www.amec.com) has recently been awarded an evergreen contract by British Petroleum (BP) to provide "recurring baseload services" to BP's refinery in Coryton, Essex (UK). The wide scope of this contract comprises engineering, purchasing, and project management services for that location.

AMEC does not disclose the advance notice time of that contract, but its purpose is obvious. BP realizes that in order to replace AMEC it would have to perform a multitude of supplier selection tasks for various tasks and projects over an extended period of time. For that, search costs would be enormous. Placing that responsibility into the hands of a service provider with a proven track record (AMEC has built and serviced many refineries throughout the world) reduces search costs significantly. This is BP's payoff for lock-in.

Motivating customers to sign long-term contracts can be difficult. In order to provide significant savings in search costs, long-term suppliers must be able to provide a range of services and products that eliminates the need for customers to deal with multiple sources. Procurement of complex services such as engineering and project management are search cost intensive and, thus, present higher cost savings through permanent outsourcing. The AMEC case points in that direction.

Summary: The Role of Contracts in B2B Transactions

Overall, contracts play a major role in B2B transactions to reduce the risk that arises from partner-specific investment. A car maker that has a single seat supplier with JIT capability or a retailer that requires expensive and proprietary IOS-investment are only examples for such investments. Their purpose is always the same: partner-specific investment into location or IT-infrastructure makes exchanges much more efficient but at the same time introduces significant risk. Such partners can't be exchanged on short notice.

The contract then serves primarily as an instrument to reduce the risk of such arrangements. For example, you agree on conducting transactions for a longer period of time in order to recoup partner-specific investment, or you agree on penalties if some party does not do what it is supposed to. The problem is that contracts can't completely eliminate the risk in arrangements with partner-specific investment. Every contract is incomplete because every possible contingency cannot be foreseen and the contract designed accordingly.

Contractual Lock-in in B2C

In business-to-consumers transactions long-term contracts are rarely needed to safeguard parties against opportunistic behavior or to reduce the customer's search costs.[4] Vendors need them to cover account set-up costs.

Firms such as banks, ISPs or mobile phone service providers must bear significant account set-up costs. In the mobile phone industry, experts estimate setup costs at $250–300.[5] They are necessary to create an account in the company's data bank, register and verify customer data, and facilitate invoicing.

Vendors often try to recoup some part of account set-up costs by entry fee pricing. An entry fee is a one-time charge to cover one-time set-up costs. Many industries are so competitive that entry fees don't come close to set-up costs. In this case, long-term contracts provide an incentive to bear set-up costs that cannot be recouped completely by entry fees. A long-term contract increases the probability of sufficient revenues from a customer to cover the set-up costs.

---

4 Here is an exception: Long-term rental agreements between landlord and tenant provide an incentive for the tenant to invest into the house or apartment because she knows that the tenant will stay longer.
5 These significant set-up costs motivated suppliers to the mobile phone industry to develop self-service set-up and activation technologies reducing set-up costs by 10% or $30–40. See: http://www.verisign.com/corporate/news/2003/pr_20030317c_print.html.

Loyalty Rewards—but Better Beware!

Over the last few years, we have seen an inflation of various types of bonus point programs. Bonus points are incentives for sustained customer loyalty. Frequent flyer programs (FFP) are the textbook example. FFP are based on accumulated purchase volume. This means that bonus points are awarded on the basis of the purchase volume accumulated over a certain period of time. With AAdvantage, you need 25,000 AA traveler miles for a continental round-trip ticket. Typically travelers accumulate the 25,000 miles over several flights, which is an incentive to stay loyal.

This means that companies buy customer loyalty. It does not matter whether a "cash back" bonus, a complimentary flight to a destination of your choice, or some other freebie is offered. What matters is that customers realize being loyal and accumulating purchases is something they do in order to get something for free later.

It seems that today everybody offers bonus points in some way. However, many of these programs are faulty by design. It is not easy to play the "Bonus Point Game" right. It is so important to understand the economics of accumulated volume discounts.

WHAT ARE ACCUMULATED VOLUME DISCOUNTS?

You would be hard pressed to find a B2B supplier who does not offer volume discounts. They also proliferate for consumer products. With a volume discount you pay less per unit when you buy more ("Buy two, get one free"). Volume discounts are intended to increase purchasing volume with every order the buyer places. If effective, the buyer places fewer but larger orders. Larger orders increase sales and production efficiency. The buyer, however, does not necessarily consume more.

With regard to switching costs, simple volume discounts don't do the trick. For volume discounts to create switching costs they must be based on cumulative purchases: the more a customer has bought in the past, the higher the discount she receives with the next purchase from the same supplier.

> Intel has found a nice way to implement a very effective loyalty incentive system on the basis of accumulated purchases. And it does so even without offering discounts! Intel is in a market with rapidly declining prices for new generations of processors. Being able to equip new PCs with the newest Intel processor means that PC makers can—for some time—command higher prices in the market. For them, it is paramount to be "in the market" as early as possible. Selling new PCs with a processor that has been on the market for a year is less profitable. Therefore, Intel ships its newest processor only to those customers who have accumulated high purchasing volumes in the past. These customers can sell this product at higher prices than those customers not on the early shipment list.

Accumulation of purchases means that companies create a link between past and future purchases. Simple volume discounts cannot achieve that. When past purchases are the driver of future discounts, customers have a strong incentive to stay loyal.

In general, every system in which customers are offered volume discounts on the basis of accumulated purchases provides an incentive to stick to a certain supplier. They differ along the following criteria.

- when the discounts are offered—*initially* ("up front") with the first purchase, or after a certain number of purchases have been made ("back-end")
- the kind of discounts offered—cash refund, goods or services, and so on.
- their time span—how long are bonus points valid?
- whether they are product- or brand-specific, or are based on the monetary volume of all purchases from a supplier

UP-FRONT LOYALTY DISCOUNTS AND SOME LESSONS FROM INDUSTRY

In the European mobile phone industry, it is common practice to attract customers into one- or two-year service contracts with substantial discounts on new mobile phones or by waiving the fixed monthly service fee for a couple of months. Initially, customers pay less for the service, but they are locked-in for an extended period of time.

Up-front discounts are usually linked to a long-term contractual agreement that provides lock-in. This contractual lock-in is necessary to assure a stream of revenues to pay for the discount. But even with contractual lock-in, up-front discounts can suffer from serious problems.

Risky Revenue Streams

From the vendor's perspective, contractual lock-in is necessary to reduce the uncertainty of pay-back on the discount. Despite the contract providing customer lock-in, the profitability of the up-front discount model is risky.

Let's look again at mobile phones. Many customers pay a flat monthly service fee and non-negative charges per minute for every call (they can be zero). Thus, for the length of the contract, the service provider receives a more or less certain cash flow from monthly service fees. This cash flow is partly necessary to recover the initial discount. To what extent recovery is possible depends on the type of contract the customer signs (low monthly fee, high airtime charges, or vice versa) and the actual use of the service (airtime). The return on the discount is high if the customer pays a high monthly fee and uses the mobile phone a lot.

In Germany, as in other mature mobile phone markets, the share of customers signing contracts with a fixed monthly service fee has declined progressively. It is more or less limited to business users. Today, 60% of 65 million German subscribers use the prepaid option with no monthly service fee but higher airtime charges. For service providers, the share of revenues coming from risk-free price elements (the monthly service fee) has significantly decreased. As a result, the risk of service providers offering up-front discounts has increased. It becomes more risky to offer up-front discounts if future revenues are more uncertain. This has led service providers to:

- limit substantial up-front discounts to service contracts with higher monthly fees (business customers),
- introduce discounted, yet expensive, new phone models to customers who prefer the prepaid option later, after their prices have declined,
- reduce the discount. German vendors discounted a new 2-year contract by roughly €200 during the 1990s. The average discount today is significantly lower.

This example demonstrates that the profitability of up-front discounts heavily depends on the pricing model even with contractual lock-in. A model in which the vendor bears much of the uncertainty associated with the return on the discount is critical. This happens if the customer generates a volatile stream of revenues.

A pricing model providing a fairly stable stream of revenues is necessary to justify up-front discounts:

- increase the share of revenues originating from fixed service fees ("flat rates"),
- introduce a minimum consumption requirement, and/or
- limit marketing to customer groups with low volatility in consumption.

Attracting the Wrong Customers

Large up-front discounts may attract the wrong customers. Wrong customers buy the subsidized "teaser" (a game console plus one or two games), but do not buy enough complementary products (additional games). They are attracted by low entry prices but their interest or income is not sufficient to sustain their role as a constant source of revenues. Then, up-front discounts produce high churn rates.

This problem is similar to the problem of selecting customers with less volatile consumption. But here we are concerned with the problem of whether customers attracted by low entry prices consume enough *at all*. The same solution applies: be more selective with your target market when providing up-front discounts. Be sure to target customers that will be providing enough revenues in the future.

Interaction with Loyalty Programs

Up-front discounts intended to attract new customers and extend the customer base may interact unfavorably with instruments to increase the loyalty of existing customers. Consider the AOL case:

In recent years, subscriber growth at AOL seems to have come primarily from promotion programs in which new customers were offered several months of free AOL service. In many cases, new AOL customers buy new PCs bundled with free AOL service for 3 or 4 months. According to industry analysts, the average monthly subscription revenue of AOL is about $17 per subscriber per month.[1] The regular service charge is $23.90. This indicates that many AOL customers pay nothing at all—at least for some time. CNET reports: "Certain PC makers, such as Gateway, offer free AOL service for certain time periods to new computer buyers. When someone signs up for the AOL deal, AOL pays the PC maker a bounty fee and the PC maker pays AOL a monthly fee up to the amount of an AOL subscription."

Offering several months of free service on sign-up is a classic case of up-front discounts. In this case, it has led to a significant decline in revenue growth for AOL.

What makes this strategy critical is negative interaction with AOL's "Member Savings" program. This is a program designed to keep AOL customers from changing their internet service provider. However, 34 million AOL subscribers buy new PC hardware every 3–4 years, for example, 8–10 million each year. PC dealers cannot discriminate between AOL customers and others. If free service is part of an otherwise attractive bundle, "old" AOL customers terminate their AOL account (for which they pay $23.90 a month) when the buy a new Gateway PC only to return as a "new" AOL customer with free service.

This interaction between acquisition and loyalty instruments creates a "revolving-door customer" who has provided significant revenues in the past and now leaves, only to return with a cheaper or even free service plan. This really is a pesky problem and worries analysts (see Figure 9-1). In effect, the customer base is unchanged, but the average subscription fee declines. Clearly, there is interaction between up-front discounts to sign up new customers and member savings programs: one affects the other. In this case, the reason for the negative interaction is that it is impossible to discriminate against old customers when tying freebies to the sales of new PCs. Managers should be aware of this possibility and design loyalty instruments accordingly.

There is an important lesson in this case.

Acquisition and loyalty programs should not be handled independently from each other. Customers whose contractual lock-in has expired may be aware of discounts offered to new customers. A program to keep existing customers "on board" can be hurt if up-front discounts intended for new customers are offered in an indiscriminate fashion. True first-time buyers must be identified reliably and sign-up incentives designed to discriminate against old customers.

---

1 See: http://news.zdnet.co.uk/story/0,,t269-s2106641,00.html.

For AOL, Free Service May Be Costly

Analysts Worry That Company's Giveaways Are Hurting Its Bottom Line

With Fewer 'Newbies,' Tried-and-True Sign-Up Schemes Are Faltering

By JULIA ANGWIN
Staff Reporter of THE WALL STREET JOURNAL

UNTIL AUGUST, Sam Morgan was paying America Online $23.90 (€27.30) a month. Since then, the 44-year-old resident of Rochester, New York, hasn't paid a thing, even though he uses the service regularly.

That's because he bought a new Gateway computer that came with a year's worth of free America Online service. So he switched off his old account and started a new free account. When it expires this August, he says, "I may start paying again, or I am thinking of possibly moving on."

He isn't the only one. It appears that fewer and fewer of AOL Time Warner Inc.'s America Online subscribers are paying full fare. Analyst Mary Meeker at Morgan Stanley estimates the percentage of nonpaying U.S. subscribers jumped to 15% this year from 7% a year earlier.

The online service rocketed past rivals in the 1990s with its formula of blanketing America with sign-up discs offering a period of free service, then converting the users to paying customers.

That strategy was supposed to provide the growth engine for the combined AOL Time Warner, but that growth slowed recently. Earlier this week, AOL shares fell 4% when it announced it reached 34 million members at a pace slower than Wall Street had expected.

America Online Chief Executive Barry Schuler says the company's growth rate is on track, but that the characteristics of the market have changed now that about two-thirds of U.S. consumers have Internet access. "Things are going to change with the last third of the market," he says. "But you don't want to sit back and say, 'Well, because it costs more money, we don't want them.' The game is to build the base, because the one thing we have proven over time is that we will sell them lots of other things."

But now, Wall Street is wondering whether the price of that marketing gambit is too high. Last year, America Online's revenue per U.S. subscriber dropped 6%, despite a 9% price increase and a 12% rise in advertising. Last month, Lehman Bros. analyst Holly Becker downgraded AOL's stock, saying that "we believe the price increase is not sticking ... as AOL is offering new subscribers more aggressive discounts and promotions."

Michael E. Gallant, an analyst at CIBC World Markets, also downgraded the stock, based in part on concern that there are fewer new Internet users for America Online to woo.

Indeed, America Online has extended its free trials. The ubiquitous CDs used to offer a free 30-day trial; last year, the company extended it to a 45-day offer. Starting in 1999, the company began offering even longer free trials through its "bundling" arrangements with computer makers, which load the AOL software on new PCs. Gateway Inc. offers a full year of free America Online service, while Dell Computer Corp. offers six months free and Compaq Computer Corp. three months.

Generally, America Online pays the computer maker a fee for placement while the computer maker pays America Online a discounted rate for the Internet service. Frequently, these deals don't add to America Online's sales during the trial period, the company says.

Mike Kelly, America Online's chief operating officer, says the freebies, both from PC bundling and sign-up discs, are part of a deliberate strategy that pays off when many of the free users convert to paying customers. "We're very pleased with the conversion rate," he says, though he declines to disclose the figure.

The conversion rates are higher for the longer free-trial periods, an AOL spokeswoman says.

Mr. Kelly adds that America Online doesn't pay much attention to the revenue-per-subscriber number that Wall Street is focused on. "I focus on our overall profitability," Mr. Kelly says. Yet according to the company's own measures, the America Online division's operating profit margin shrank last year to 24% from 25% in 2000, due in part to aggressive marketing in Europe.

Mr. Kelly says the percentage of new AOL subscribers coming from bundles decreased in the past year, compared with the prior year. He declined to give a figure.

Historically, the bundle was a good way for America Online to reach its target market: "newbies," or people new to computing and the Internet. But these days, computer buyers are more likely to be upgrading their computers than buying their first PC.

IDC researcher Roger Kay estimates that the percentage of first-time PC buyers in the U.S. fell to 31% in 2001 from 41% in 2000. The trend is expected to continue; Mr. Kay predicts that only 7% of PC purchasers will be first-time buyers by 2006.

"Most PC buyers today, who are on their second, third, or fourth system, already have an access service and are not anxious to pay for a new one," says Mr. Kay.

America Online says bundling is one of many marketing tools for getting people to try its service.

Figure 9-1: WSJ Article on AOL Giveaways
(Reprinted with permission)

Summary

Each up-front discount companies give away is an investment into an individual customer. This investment must provide a satisfactory return. If the pricing model has a variable component, the return is uncertain. Contractual lock-in alone may not be enough to achieve a satisfying ROI on the front-end discount. Uncertainty is lower if the part of the stream of revenues coming from the customer that are predetermined can be enlarged.

BACK-END LOYALTY DISCOUNTS

Frequent flyer programs are a typical case of back-end discount programs. FFPs offer incentives (for example, free travel, hotel or rental car vouchers) that have a significant value for the customer. With back-end discounts, customers initially pay higher prices in order to receive a discount later. This is a model in which there is little or no risk resulting from loyalty incentives. The customer qualifies for the discount only if her accumulated consumption is sufficient.

Back-end discount programs are by no means limited to airlines although they have played a vital role in developing successful loyalty programs. Here are examples from other industries:[2]

- HHonors was the first application of loyalty reward programs to the hotel industry (www.hhonors.com). Hilton considers it the most successful marketing instrument of the last 20 years.
- Athletic shows and apparel cataloger Road Runner Sports (www.roadrunnersports.com) offers a Run America Club membership at $19.95 a year. Members receive a 5% discount on all purchases, upgraded shipping, and a "Wear-it-and-Love-it Guarantee," among other incentives. Note that customers must spend at least $400 a year at Road Runner to break even on the membership.
- On-line bicycle store www.performancebicycles.com offers 10 points for every dollar spent. 1,000 points qualify for a $10 discount with the next purchase. Effectively, this leads to a 10% discount with two purchases of $100. Similar models have been implemented by many companies.

Mechanics of Back-end Loyalty Programs

Let us look at FFP to understand the mechanics of back-end loyalty programs. As depicted in Figure 9-2, with each regular fare, travelers receive miles that accumulate in their frequent flyer account. Additional points come with another purchase. Typically, the number of points or miles differs with the value of each purchase. The accumulation of bonus points follows a step-function. Customers take the next step with the next purchase or air travel that qualifies for bonus points. Since customers are usually free to decide when and what to buy (note the exception of book clubs), the length and height of each step will vary.

Customers are often free to decide when and which incentive they choose. With every incentive from the program, the number of bonus points is reduced. In Figure 9-2, this "discount received" happens twice. The first time, all bonus points are consumed; the second time, some are left. Note that bonus points may expire.

---

2 Taken from: http://catalogagemag.com/ar/marketing_best_catalog_loyalty/.

A customer who decides to consume all bonus points is back to zero. With regard to the loyalty program, she is a new customer. At this point, she may be indifferent between alternative suppliers and their FFP. This is a critical moment since there is no longer an incentive to stay loyal.

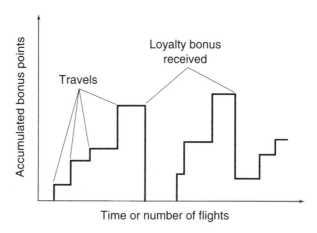

Figure 9-2: Bonus Point Example

Cash Fast-forwarding

One of the most striking features of back-end discounts is that customers pay higher prices in order to qualify for a discount later. Compared to up-front discounts, this is a much more elegant model. It reduces the risk for the vendor because the discount follows consumption and not vice versa. With the back-end model, it is the customer who invests into the sustained seller-buyer relationship, not the vendor.

There are different ways to implement back-end discounts and charge initial premiums.

- Some companies charge an entry fee that the customer can compare to the benefits that are accessible through the fee. At Road Runner Sports, every customer can decide whether the incentives offered are worth $19.95 per year. With this model, customers are required to make a club membership decision.
- Airlines don't charge entry fees, they simply charge more per flight. This is a "pay as you go" model. It does not require a membership decision from the customer. The *accumulated* price premiums are the basis for discounts.

For the customer, the entry fee model requires some knowledge about future demand. Customers must think about their future needs when making a decision about club membership. If future needs are uncertain, the entry fee is a hurdle. With the pay-as-you-go model this is not necessary and it is a more flexible model, in which customers can terminate their "membership" any time by either consuming their miles or forsaking the price premiums paid up to this point. Both models change the order of discounts and price premiums compared to up-front discounts. Price premiums come first, discounts later.

Should Bonus Points Expire?

An important decision with regard to the design of back-end loyalty programs refers to the question of whether bonus points should expire or not and when. It's an important decision because expiration puts pressure on the customer and can be a source of severe dissatisfaction. Think of a frequent and brand-loyal business traveler who plans a family trip only to find out that some of his old miles have expired leaving him short of the necessary number of bonus miles for everybody.

In the 1990s it was common practice among the bigger airlines that bonus miles would expire after three years. The idea was that miles with an expiration date would motivate customers to increase an airline's share-of-wallet or travel more by air. Consumers would try to gain the critical mass of miles faster—and before some of their valuable miles expired.

Recently, many airlines have changed that policy and now offer "eternal miles." These bonus miles are valid as long as the customer's account is active.

A third option is the hybrid model which—in the case of airlines—has no expiration date on miles as long as the customer shows some minimum level of activity.[3] This can be a certain number of flights or purchases per year.

The hybrid model can be preferable for a variety of reasons:

1. "Eternal" miles put less pressure on customers to increase a vendor's share-of-wallet or consume more. They appeal to the customer who doesn't have to worry about mileage expiration, but are less attractive for the company.

---

[3] See http://frequentflier.com/ffp-expire.htm for a more detailed discussion of this subject.

2. Expiration dates are difficult to sustain in a competitive environment. This is what happened to airlines. The first big player that sheds this policy puts a lot of pressure on others to follow. It is against consumers' interest.
3. The hybrid model can put equivalent pressure on consumers to stay brand-loyal without expiration of miles.

Implementing a hybrid discount model can be done in different ways.

- Specify some level of activity that is important to you because it saves costs or gives you a chance for cross- or up-selling. This could be a visit to the shop or the website, or some minimum level of patronage. If a customer is active with regard to these activities, bonus points should not expire. This policy reflects your appreciation of the customer's activity, but it is also conducive to your chances of increasing revenues.
- Create different types of bonus points. Following is a successful example.

Lufthansa differentiates between status miles and bonus miles. Status miles give access to special services such as luxury lounge access. Status miles expire at the end of the year. Bonus miles never expire. Lufthansa business travelers may be more interested in their status than the number of bonus miles. If this is so, then there is strong lock-in without bonus mile expiration. Clearly, the success of this model depends on customers' relative preference of status versus bonus miles

Different types of bonus points allow for more differentiation. Differentiation always provides additional profits in heterogeneous markets.

Choose the Right Incentive!

Consumption follows back-end discounts incentives. Although the term "discount" suggests that the incentive for sustained loyalty is a cash return or some other monetary equivalent, many companies don't do that—for a good reason.

Airlines are a good example. For bonus miles, customers don't get cash back, they can get a free flight. This is an excellent discount model in a fixed-cost intensive industry with low marginal costs per unit: It is very expensive to fly an airplane from A to B; it is very cheap to have another person on board. There is a huge difference between the marginal costs of a free flight and its market price. The only thing that should not happen is that a bonus point passenger competes with a regular passenger for a seat.

The idea is that a good incentive is one with significant value to the customer but with low marginal costs. To offer a cost-effective incentive is easy in fixed-cost intensive service industries such as theme parks or hotels. It is more difficult in industries with high marginal costs.

Another point to consider is the transparency of cash discounts. From the customer's point of view, cash discounts can be easily compared to competitive offers. Transparency does not work in favor of a company because it increases competition. Also, the value of a cash discount is the same to all customers.

Thus, look closely at what customers value. Indeed, some might not value a discount on the next unit of consumption at all—even if this discount is 100%. Some people don't get the idea of traveling a lot on airplanes to get a free airplane ride. Some customers prefer gaining status, which might be cheap to offer. The highest status you can achieve with Lufthansa is being a "Senator." This status will get a flier on a sold-out plane with a long waiting list on short notice. To Lufthansa, this costs little, but it is priceless to the customer. In the best case, Lufthansa says "sorry" to another person on the waiting list. In the worst case, it buys the lowest bidder out of his seat.[4] Most Lufthansa Senators are very eager to keep their status and some even buy extra miles to keep that privilege.

SUMMARY

Bonus point programs offer incentives for loyalty. Incentives cost money. In return, you get greater customer loyalty and from that increased revenues. The big question is, under what circumstances does this model pay off? Can offering discounts for loyalty become a zero-sum game?

Yes, they can and companies should be aware of that.

In part 1, we discussed the economics of switching costs and how they drive customer equity. In the case of FFP, bonus miles allow for effective price discrimination against customers who col-

---

4 Note the auction model airlines use to free a seat: gate agents call a price that increases until the passenger with the lowest price threshold signals his or her willingness to trade his/her ticket for a hotel voucher or some money and a ticket for the next day.

lect miles. This means that companies can raise prices—sometimes significantly—for the discount offered.

Incentives for loyalty can become a negative-sum game if up-front discounts are offered in the form of reduced entry prices. In markets with switching costs, reduced entry prices are not intended to attract customers with a low reservation price—which is what companies usually want with low prices.

Low entry prices in a market with switching costs are intended to attract as many high-reservation price customers as possible[5] which at the same time have significant demand for follow-up purchases. This customer type offers a potential for profitable price discrimination in the future and provides the pay-back on entry discounts.

However, with entry discounts, low-reservation price customers are always attracted. These customers don't come back because they are unwilling or unable to pay the higher prices in later periods. They will not buy again in the following periods.

From that principle, these guidelines for profitable bonus point programs follow.

1. As a vendor, don't look at customer's single purchases, but at the stream of purchases by individual customers that you wish to trigger by offering loyalty discounts. Looking at initial purchases alone can be highly misleading. If cherry pickers (low-reservation price customers) are attracted en masse, there will be no follow-up purchases to make discounts profitable. Look at the ROI of the purchase stream of individual customers attracted by loyalty discounts.

2. To forecast this ROI, companies need to know how profitable customers react to first-period discounts. If they react rationally, they will anticipate that discounts are followed by higher prices. They will be more concerned with future purchases than the initial purchase and become less price-sensitive. This may lead customers not to react to up-front discounts the way companies want.

3. Be selective with up-front discounts that are supposed to trigger follow-up purchases at higher prices. Identify those customers—or groups of them—that have sufficient willingness-to-pay for a *program*. Offer up-front discounts to them only if possible.

---

5 See P. Klemperer: Markets with Consumer Switching Costs, Quarterly Journal of Economics, May 1987, 390.

4. Such customers may be difficult to find. It helps if they cluster in certain regional areas or prefer distinctive channels of distribution. Analyze the size of the target market. Is it large enough? If not, rethink the approach.

A lot of money can be thrown away with "discounts for loyalty" programs. In the case of up-front discounts, it pays to be rigorous and analyze the target market in depth before offering rebates. Remember that it is very beneficial to be able to restrict the availability of discounts to desired customers, and not others. Back-end discounts are much less problematic and offer better potential for a positive-sum game. Companies do not have the problem of attracting customers they don't want because of the higher entry price. Customers will self-select. They join your program based on their price reservation. Since there are initially higher prices, the customers attracted will have higher willingness-to-pay.

Austrian Cordial-Group (www.cordial.at) has created a new niche in the European travel industry by employing these rather simple guidelines. Cordial operates eight luxurious resort hotels in Austria and Italy and has alliance partners in Spain, Australia, in the Caribbean and Hawaii. A traveler can't directly book a room; rather, they must buy points. Whoever wants to stay in one of Cordial's hotels must first become a Cordial club member. Cordial charges an €8,550 entry fee for which new club members receive 1,500 points. Currently, 1,500 points translate into eight weeks of vacation time at a hotel of choice for a family of two adults and two children during holiday season (13 weeks during off-season).

In the highly competitive European travel industry, this approach is vastly different to the dominant low-price strategy. Cordial reasons that customers willing to pay more than $9,000 up front are both affluent and able to do the math. Club members are a rather exclusive group, which is something they like. On average, an overnight stay costs €110 per person which is an excellent deal considering the quality offered. Wary customers might be concerned about having to go to the same place again and again, but the selection among many club hotels offers variety. Also, points have a 10-year expiration time. Customers are not forced to spend every vacation at a Cordial resort.

The high entry fee will result in customers who don't look at a single vacation, but at a series of vacation *programs*. After all, who can afford eight-week vacations? Thus, customers' incentive to stay loyal in order to break even on the non-refundable entry fee is significant.

10

Innovate for Technological Lock-in

Technological lock-in rests upon a proprietary technology that forces customers to buy repeatedly from the same vendor. If coupled with a large customer base, the profit implications are staggering, as Carl Shapiro and Hal Varian note.

> "The great fortunes of the information age lie in the hands of companies that have successfully established proprietary architectures that are used by a large installed base of locked-in customers. And many of the biggest headaches of the information age are visited upon companies that are locked-in to information systems that are inferior, orphaned, or monopolistically supplied."[1]

With durable purchases, technological lock-in can be very powerful. The longer a customer expects to use a new product, the longer she is locked-in with regard to upgrades or follow-up purchases of spare parts and complements. Again, look at the HP printer case: The proprietary technological interface between the HP printer and the printer cartridges (an indispensable component that is repeatedly purchased) creates technological lock-in that, in turn, produces a staggering potential for price premiums on supplies.

Technological lock-in refers to a situation in which the customer's wish for compatibility between different purchases creates brand-loyalty. Once the decision has been made to adopt Microsoft Windows, it is preferable to buy Windows-based application software. The same holds for telecommunication systems or Mattel's Barbie. Other examples are game consoles and games. In such a system, all complementary components must work together. One way to ensure this is to standardize the technological interfaces

---

1 Excerpt from C. Shapiro and H.R. Varian: Information Rules: A Guide to the Network Economy, Harvard Business School Press 1999.

between the components. We find that very often in the IT hardware industry. Connecting peripherals to PCs or notebooks is easy because the interfaces (serial, parallel, USB or others) are standardized. Then, different system elements can be bought from different vendors. In a way, refill manufacturers standardize the interface between ink and the printer. Since they specialize in refilling all types of used cartridges with generic ink, they eliminate the technological barrier created by printer suppliers.

Companies can also design the interfaces between the components of a system in a proprietary way. Then, the system can only be used if all components are from the same vendor. This creates technological lock-in when components are bought after the initial purchase of the first system component has been made.

Creating technological lock-in raises a number of important questions.

1. What are the economic implications of technological lock-in?
2. In what kind of situation is technological lock-in better than an "open source" policy?
3. What kind of company is able to impress a technological lock-in regime on a market?

IMPLICATIONS OF TECHNOLOGICAL LOCK-IN

Technological lock-in creates loyal customers in the market for proprietary supplies, spare parts, upgrades or complements of a system. If a person owns a GSM mobile phone and wishes to use it for mobile internet access, he needs a GSM phone card for the notebook. No other system will do. This means that once a proprietary system has been adopted, it is highly probable that the consumer will be brand-loyal (system-loyal) with related purchases in the future.

To a large extent, technological lock-in lies in the discretion of the vendor. You can decide to practice an "open source" policy which enables other companies to sell components to your system. You can also license knowledge to competitors (which is what Matsushita did with VHS), or keep it proprietary and exclude everybody else from using it commercially. Technological lock-in results from the decision to keep technological interfaces between the components of a system proprietary. Two important implications result from that decision.

1. The customer is locked-in with regard to future purchases. This lock-in is valid until there is demand for complements or upgrades for a specific system and its components. Thus, it is temporary.
2. This decision makes the adoption of a proprietary system—especially if it is new and unproven—risky. Customers must believe that spare parts, complements, and upgrades will be available from the same supplier when they will be needed. This risk slows the adoption of technology with lock-in.

Technological Lock-in Is Temporary

Innovation renders even established technologies with strong lock-in obsolete. It may happen sooner or later, but it always happens. Brian Arthur of the Santa Fe Institute said the following about the duration of technological lock-in:[2]

> "The fact is, technology comes in waves. No one I know . . . says that lock-in is forever. We are locked-in to English, temporarily. In 500 years' time, it'll be a different language. Three hundred years ago people were locked into Latin as the international means of discourse. No one said a lock-in is forever. In fact, it's taken for granted in high tech that lock-ins typically last anywhere between a year or two and five years."

Markets with technological lock-in are more sluggish in changing from one proprietary system to another. This creates a potential for additional profits for the dominant supplier. But economists believe that the higher profits from the lock-in of a large customer base are, the stronger are the incentives for competitors to invent and come up with a new technology that is so superior that customers will bear even high switching costs. It has happened with vinyl records, black-and-white TVs, and it will, eventually, happen to Microsoft Windows.[3]

The duration of technological lock-in very much depends on the speed of innovation in an industry. In an industry with short

---

2 See: http://www.pretext.com/may98/columns/intview.htm.
3 Call me an optimist, but is has begun: In early 2003, the city of Munich, Germany, decided to get rid of Windows and install Linux complete with Linux-based office software on all of its 14,000 PCs in city administration. When this became apparent, even Steve Balmer showed up to keep the city's mayor from defecting to the enemy. He offered to cut the price significantly, but to no avail. Munich's mayor, Christian Ude, was quoted saying that the move "championed the use of Linux as a way to cut back on Munich's dependence on a single IT vendor and a way to spur competition."

technology cycles (IT hardware), lock-in can be as short as a year or two. For commercial airplanes, it is much longer. This is because companies like Boeing and Airbus have little incentive to innovate fast if they need 10–15 years to make a profit on a new generation of airplanes.

Adoption Is Risky

From the customer's perspective, adopting a technology with strong lock-in is a bet that the supplier is still out there when she needs him and that the supplier delivers the products and services at attractive prices. Early buyers of SAP's R3 ERP system successfully bet on SAP to deliver all the components and services needed to run this software as intended. Customers of the many software suppliers that did not survive the shakeout were in for an unpleasant surprise.

The perceived risk of adopting a proprietary system depends on a number of factors such as the following:

- *characteristics of the supplier*—risk is reduced if the supplier has a broad customer base that allows for sustainable development of its technology. For the same reason, it decreases with a stronger financial base.
- *characteristics of the adopter*—a larger customer can bear more risk than a smaller one. Bigger customers may adopt several systems simultaneously in order to spread risk over several suppliers. This is why bigger companies are often earlier adopters of technology with lock-in.
- *speed of innovation*—faster innovation reduces risk because alternative technologies are available earlier.

Innovations with technological lock-in will not be adopted if the customer's perceived risk of adoption is too high in relation to its benefits. The easiest way to reduce adoption risk is to practice an "open source" policy that may motivate competitors to adopt the same technology, resulting in more than one supplier "fuelling" the system and reducing or even eliminating customer lock-in. The "go-it-alone" strategy is to try to lock-in customers technologically. But this requires positioning a company and brand as one that poses little or acceptable adoption risk. Companies with a broad customer base, such as SAP or IBM, are in a good position to do that. Others, especially smaller and start-up companies, find that difficult.

An alliance strategy is one in which partners collaborate to engage in promoting a new and proprietary technology. The advantage is that the more companies promote a certain technology, the less risky is its adoption by the customers. Matsushita has done exactly that by licensing its new VHS technology in the 1970s to virtually "every comer." Ironically, Sony invited JVC and Matsushita to license Betamax in 1974, which they refused.

What is the trade-off? With an alliance strategy, the probability of the success of a new technology is increased because there is less adoption risk due to reduced customer lock-in. Even after the initial purchase (for example, for Windows), customers can buy complements such as office application software from other vendors. Because of that there will be more users of specific technology around, but the share of them is less than 100%. With the "go-it-alone" strategy, the market share with users of specific technology is 100%, but there will be less users because of the higher risk.

TECHNOLOGICAL LOCK-IN IN NETWORK MARKETS

Sometimes technological lock-in results from the installed base of a certain technology. Think of VHS and Betamax. At any time in the race between the two systems, VHS cassettes had longer recording times. When VHS was introduced in 1976 by Matsushita, its cassettes could hold two hours, which was a crucial advantage against Betamax with its one hour recording capacity. What movie is only 60 minutes long?

Because of this advantage, VHS collected market share faster than Betamax, creating a network effect. Higher market share of VHS translated into more rental and other commercial movies being available on VHS cassettes, simply because there were more people with that system to sell to. This fueled even higher demand—a positive feedback loop on market share for Matsushita. Today, Betamax is long gone.[4]

A network market is a market in which a product's benefit to a single user depends on the number of all users. The more users, the more utility consumers derive from a product. Classic examples are phones, fax machines, and video systems. The network effect creates lock-in on the market level. A rather small market

---

4 Sometimes, people confuse Betamax with Betacam, which is Sony's professional recording system. This system was introduced 1982.

share advantage (as with VHS in the 1970s) translates into market dominance because of the positive feedback loop. Microsoft has become big this way.

Such markets can become *path dependent*.[5] There is only one limit to the growth of a certain company: the number of potential users in the market. Path-dependency creates strong lock-in for customers and suppliers. It is much better to buy and stick to a technology that everybody else has. Technological lock-in in network markets results from the installed base, not prior purchases of individual customers. This is the difference to the printer case. HP is more concerned with individual lock-in because of prior purchases into a proprietary system—independent from the number of users.

INNOVATION STRATEGY

Technological lock-in is a strategy for innovative companies. It requires a focus on new and proprietary technological solutions that replace an inferior, but established solution. The most important resource for a technological lock-in strategy is superior R&D. Managing R&D is one of the toughest managerial problems. Numerous empirical studies have been conducted to find the success factors of "good" R&D. Robert Cooper of the Product Development Institute (see www.prod-dev.com) is regarded as one of the leading world experts on the success factors of new product development. He considers the following factors among the key determinants of R&D success:[6]

1. Seeking clearly differentiated and unique products with superior customer value. This requires heavy and constant involvement of customers and their needs in the new product development (NPD) process.
2. Developing the customer needs and the competitive situation comes first: It is an essential part of the "up-front homework" that is needed before any serious development work should be started.

---

5 See B. Arthur: Competing Technologies, Increasing Returns, and Lock-in by Historical Small Events, in: Increasing Returns and Path Dependence in the Economy, edited by B. Arthur, University of Michigan Press, 2000, 13–32.
6 Source: http://www.prod-dev.com/pdf/Working_Paper_10.pdf.

3. A sharp, early and stable product definition including the target market definition, the benefits delivered, the positioning including price and product features.
4. Proper execution of the market launch—with enough resources.
5. Clearly defined go/kill-stages throughout the NPD process.
6. Motivated cross-functional teams with support from top management.

Aiming for technological lock-in means that superior value and the business case describing possible market reaction become even more important. The benefits that technology promises to offer must clearly outweigh the adoption risk of a new and proprietary technology. Since customers will always look at alternative suppliers (that possibly pose less risk), the business case should look closely at the competitive situation in terms of relative adoption risk.

Creating Switching Costs through the Customer-Supplier Relationship

Relationship marketing (RM) has repeatedly been proposed as the new marketing paradigm and as being the cornerstone of a superior customer-centered strategy. As with many new, and possibly fruitful, concepts, relationship marketing was hailed as a new paradigm substituting the "old" transaction-based thinking. This is true, but not always. The problem is that the relationship approach is sometimes not appropriate. If not, there is little potential for switching costs based on customer relationships. Maybe this is why many companies struggle with the concept and its implementation via customer relationship marketing (CRM).

WHAT HAPPENED TO RELATIONSHIP MARKETING?

At the core of RM is the idea of establishing ongoing relationships with customers. CRM comprises a set of techniques and technologies to achieve that goal.[1] Ultimately, the customer is supposed to reduce the choice to the preferred vendor or supplier. Several issues have been criticized with regard to an all-encompassing RM concept, including the following.

A relationship is a series of interrelated interactions between two parties. The typical perspective of many RM proponents is that of the vendor. They assume that the vendor is solely in charge of the relationship to the customer. In a manner of speaking, he is the pilot who decides where to fly. The customer is simply the

---

1 See: L.L. Berry: Relationship Marketing and Service Perspectives from 1983 and 2002, Journal of Relationship Marketing, vol. 1, 2002, 59–77.

passenger who needs to get on a different plane if she wants to go someplace else. Joao Proenca and Luis de Castro of the University of Porto in Portugal comment: *"This means that a relationship analyzed out of its interactive context is normally conceptualized as involving clients without any capability for action and this is contrary to the nature of relationships."*[2]

If one considers the customer as somebody who is supposed to react to CRM-based marketing instruments and there is no room to bring in unique suggestions, information, and actions by the customer, the strategy is not truly relationship-oriented. Marketing may be more sophisticated, but it is still one-sided, based on the assumption that the customer should not actively shape the relationship. Ask if customers can react to CRM activities or trigger vendor action, and does that add value to them? If not, then there is probably no relationship from the customer's point of view. There is no customer relationship until the customer feels so.[3]

The question "Does the customer want a relationship?" is rarely asked. Most customers don't really want a true relationship with, say, a car manufacturer or an airline. What they want instead is to be treated with the qualities of a good relationship when they need them. This is entirely different. One reason is that most customers like to be in charge of when interaction should occur and when not. Here is an example:

> About a year ago, my wife and I bought a Mercedes A-class from the local Mercedes-Benz dealer. About eight months after we bought the car, we received a flashy personalized mailing complete with several brochures from Daimler-Chrysler inviting us to look at new A-class models. Obviously, DC obtained our address from the dealer and has put it into its CRM database. The mailing did not include a questionnaire or any other element asking for additional information about our use of this car or further purchase intentions, etc. We were unable to react to the mailing in any way—except to buy a new A-class. I talked to a senior representative at the ad agency in charge of the mailing about this and he considered that omission to be a "small fulfillment error."

---

2 See: J. F. Proenca and L. M. de Castro: The Nature of Corporate Banking Relationships for Relationship Marketing, in: Proceedings of the 7th Conference on Relationship Marketing, Berlin, 2003, 251–266 (quote from page 263).

3 See: J.G. Barnes: Close to the Customer: But is it really a Relationship?, Journal of Marketing, 10, 1994, 561–570.

Two months later we received an even more elaborate mailing. Again, no possibility for us to react. My wife and I were amused—does DC expect us to buy a new car every year? Frankly, we don't want a relationship to DC or any other car company whose brand we happen to own. However, we do appreciate to be treated with the qualities of a good relationship in case we need the company. As long as we don't need DC, we rather prefer not to hear from them.

In many markets such as fast moving consumer goods, consumers just want transactions. There is no connection between those transactions from the customers' view and, thus, no need for a relationship with the vendor. In such markets, CRM is a useless tool because it wrongly assumes that there is a basis for relationships with customers.[4] In such industries, superior brand value and a high degree of distribution will outperform any CRM wizardry.

SWITCHING COSTS THROUGH RELATIONSHIPS TO CUSTOMERS?

Can customer-vendor relationships create switching costs? One might be doubtful, but, yes, they can! Switching costs based on relationships are emotional switching costs based on value-adding personal relationships to the supplier's representatives.

Switching costs based on personal relationships are significant in the market for medical services. Most patients are unable to evaluate the quality of the diagnosis or the medical treatment provided. In order to do that, they would need to consult another physician or become one. However, over time patients develop trust and confidence, if a physician is able to help. This development of trust and confidence leads to psychological switching costs which typically makes an established patient-doctor relationship hard to break. Empirical research indicates that the level of customer knowledge is a crucial factor. The lower it is, the more trust can create psychological switching costs.[5]

---

4 See S. Santema: Relationships in a Dyadic Perspective, Proceedings of the 7th Conference on Relationship Marketing, Berlin, 2003, 131–144.
5 See T.L. Aldershof and F.T. Schut: Switching Behavior of Consumers on Dutch Social Health Insurance, Proceedings of the 4th European Conference on Health Economics, 2002.

Emotional switching costs, or psychological switching costs as they are sometimes called, refer to non-economic bonds.[6] They arise with the creation of social and emotional bonds between buyer and seller.[7] As the example from the medical sector indicates, they play a major role in markets with "quality uncertainty." Quality is uncertain if the buyer cannot establish the quality of a product or service before buying.

Go "Direct" to Create Relationship-based Switching Costs

Emotional bonds cannot be created without personal interaction between buyer and seller. It is interesting to note that some people speak of psychological switching costs when referring to electronic business. How can that be? How can emotional bonds be created without face-to-face contact? They cannot. There is no potential for emotional bonds if an indirect sales model is used in which salespeople don't interact directly with customers.

In 1999, Germany's largest bank, Deutsche Bank, decided to rename its private banking division "Deutsche Bank 24." Parallel to that, Deutsche Bank 24 implemented an aggressive internet strategy ("e-Banking"). The idea was to substitute the costly provision of personal service by more cost-effective internet-based channels. Consequently, the number of branches was to be reduced significantly and the internet-based service capabilities to be greatly improved.

This strategy was scrapped in late 2002. Deutsche Bank found that many customers want personal service and are less prone to e-Banking than assumed. Deutsche Bank also learned that providing e-Services may be cost effective, but it eliminates any chance for the development of emotional bonds to staff members.

In banking, however, switching costs provide an important share of a brand's price premium. Therefore, you don't want to hurt your customer's commitment. Today, Deutsche Bank is basically back to where they were in early 1999, alas, minus

---

6 See: M. Hess, J.E. Ricart: Managing Customer Switching Costs: A Framework for Competing in the Network Environment, University of Nevarra Working Paper, N. 472, 2002.
7 See R. Mandhachitara, P.G. Patterson and T. Smith: Switching Costs as a Moderator of Customer Satisfaction: An Example in Thailand's Service Industry, Proceedings of the ANZMAC 2000 Conference, 767–772.

the €1 billion they invested in e-Banking and also without the emotional bonds to customers created over years.

Look at the effect of indirect sales models on psychological switching costs.

In many industries, to go direct is not an option. Breakfast cereals can't be sold profitably with a direct sales approach. Intermediaries are needed to reach such a mass market efficiently. However, in a mass market with predominance of the indirect sales model, the dealer-customer relationship may generate brand-related switching costs. Empirical research from the automobile industry indicates that dealer loyalty has a tremendous impact on brand loyalty. Many car buyers in Europe prefer to negotiate directly with a sales agent and they also prefer to deal with service personnel they know well. In this case, the dealer-customer relationship may create psychological switching costs.

Add Value through Personal Relationships

For personal relationships to become a source of switching costs, they must provide value to the customer. Personal relationships can provide significant value to the customer and thereby create switching costs.

- Personal relationships are the necessary foundation for mutual trust to develop. Trust becomes a substitute for qualified judgment when quality is uncertain. Experts do not need to be consulted or more information researched if the customer believes the vendor to be trustworthy. This can save the customer significant transaction costs. For that reason, personal relationships are an important source of switching costs in the medical services industry but at the same time reduce transaction costs.
- Emotional bonds offer a "feel good factor." Most people prefer to do business with somebody they like if the business at hand is risky. It's like walking the high-wire with a safety net. The importance of this factor is heavily influenced by the cultural background of the people involved. Empirical studies found that in Asia and the Middle East strong emphasis is placed on developing good personal relationships between partners before deals are made or contracts are signed. There, it is unthinkable to establish good business relationships without establishing personal relationships. A VP of sales at a large German construction company once said,

"One time, I was in Saudi Arabia to present my company's proposal for a large construction project on which we wanted to bid. When I met the customer for the first time, the only thing they wanted to talk about was family! We ended up showing pictures of our kids to each other. On the first meeting, we didn't talk about the project at all. They wanted to know who I am."

Establishing strong personal relationships can be crucial to success in industrial selling. Empirical research in B2B marketing has found success in personal selling to be strongly dependent on the personal characteristics of the buyer and the seller. The more similar they are, the higher the probability of success. This is called the "matching rule."

If the seller needs to be matched to the buyer, one should pay close attention to who is selling to whom. Companies need to be aware of customer types in terms of their personal characteristics and need to match sales and service people to these types. It seems that this greatly facilitates the development of good personal relationships.

It should come as no surprise that for emotional bonds to develop between members of a sales organization and customers, stability in a sales force is a crucial element. If account responsibility is regularly changed, such bonds can not develop. This takes time. Things such as job rotation and speedy promotion are wonderful but they may also hurt you.

LOOK AT THE IMPORTANCE OF RELATIONSHIPS IN CONTEXT

The propensity of customers to switch vendors is determined by many factors. Switching costs are only one of them. Others include variety seeking motives and, of course, price or quality advantages of other vendors. How important are personal relationships compared to them?

A study of relationships between commercial banks and corporate customers shows that in this industry personal relationships play a minor role when compared to seemingly "hard" issues such as price, product portfolio, or switching costs.[8] A number of

---

8 See K.H. Wathne, H. Biong and J.B. Heide: Choice of Suppliers in Embedded Markets: Relationship and Marketing Program Effects, Journal of Marketing, 65, 2001, 54–66.

reasons may be responsible for that result. First, maybe the corporate customer really—as one customer was quoted in this study—"couldn't care less about relationships." This would indicate that a personal relationship does not add value to the customer. Plus, over the last few years, many banks have tried to reduce costs by cutting service personnel and moving services to the internet or other low-cost service channels such as teller machines. This strategy aimed at service efficiency wreaks havoc with well-established personal relationships to customers. They are virtually cut off. No wonder that customers place less emphasis on relationships to the vendor—there are none left.

This is not to say that efficiency in selling and providing services should not play a role. It always does. But companies should also look at the role of personal relationships to the customer. It may be costly to maintain, but if it adds value to customers it may provide a safeguard against customer switching. Cutting customers off will increase customer switching because of lower switching costs. This is why it is important to look at customer relationships in context.

12

Creating Switching Costs: a Synopsis

There is a wide variety of instruments to create switching costs. Every instrument poses specific challenges that should be taken into account.

- Brand-specific learning by the customer must be motivated and enabled. This is achieved through idiosyncratic product features that require brand-specific training. The customer is motivated to invest in brand-specific learning if this knowledge adds sufficient value.
- Contractual lock-in is necessary to insure partner-specific investment. The contract serves as a safeguard against possible opportunistic behavior and insures sufficient revenues to cover account set-up costs.
- Bonus point programs have become increasingly popular over the last few years. Yet, they pose difficult challenges. In effect, bonus points are discounts—often in cash—that can be offered up-front or after consumption ("back-end"). These two options work very differently and must be carefully managed in order to be profitable.
- Technological lock-in arises if a company designs the interfaces between the components of a system in a proprietary way. This is the case in the game console or the ERP software industry. Technological lock-in makes adoption risky for consumers. This may slow down adoption and decrease the sales potential. It also requires the company to position itself as a partner that poses acceptable risk to the buyer.

Creating true switching costs by customer relationships is very much limited to companies dealing directly with customers. This is because face-to-face interaction is necessary for psychological or emotional switching costs to arise.

Different instruments create switching costs in different ways and result in different management issues. To create switching costs requires looking at their *enablers* (see Table 12-1). Switching costs are enabled in very different ways. With learning, it is brand idiosyncrasy (BMW's iDrive, eBay auctioning) that creates switching costs. The same principle holds for technological lock-in, which relies on idiosyncrasy in the interfaces of the components of a technology. To create switching costs on either basis may require a disruptive innovation. In a mature market with highly standardized products, there is little potential for brand-specific learning or technological lock-in. Companies would have to restart the competitive process by innovation in order for idiosyncrasy to be accepted in the market.

Binding contractual agreements and relationship-based switching costs are primarily instruments to reduce transaction costs. Both play a major role when dealings between a vendor and a customer involve significant uncertainty concerning quality or revenues. The contract serves as an instrument to safeguard the parties against foreseeable risks. A good personal relationship is the basis for successfully mediating between the parties in critical situations not covered by the contract. It is important, however, to look at relationships in context, that is, in terms of the relative importance from the customer's perspective.

SOURCE OF SWITCHING COSTS	HOW DO THEY WORK?	ENABLER	PROBLEMS
Learning	Economizing on brand-specific knowledge	Brand idiosyncrasy	• competition: standardization, and resulting pressure on necessity for learning • may need technological disruption • one time
Technology	Compatibility of related purchases ("system")	System with proprietary interfaces	Need for innovative leaps ("shocks") in mature markets, positioning
Contractual	Contracts facilitate coordination with partner-specific investment	Securing important supply sources, ensuring revenue stream to cover account set-up costs	Remaining risk of partner specific investment
Relationship	Reduction of transaction cost (driven by quality uncertainty)	Adding value through personal relationships	Relative importance of relationship received by customers ("context")
Incentive (Bonus point)	Pay-back for loyalty	Offering benefits for accumulated purchasing volume	Implementation, e.g.: • front vs. back-end • interference of acquisition and loyalty programs

Table 12-1: Overview on Instruments to Create Switching Costs

Loyalty incentives are enabled by any benefits provided to customers which link past and future purchases. Because purchasing volume is individual, so are the incentives. The benefits offered can vary (cash, bonus points, or freebies), but they must be valued by customers. The implementation of loyalty incentives is highly critical. It is difficult to make front-end discounts profitable. Front-end discounts may invite cherry-pickers and may interfere with membership programs. Back-end discounts force customers to pay price premiums first, which may present a hurdle.

Looking at industry practice, we find distinctive switching cost strategies comprising combinations of switching cost instruments.

Up-front discounts put the vendor at risk if the customer does not purchase repeatedly. Therefore, discounts should be combined with a binding contract that guarantees sufficient revenues to pay for the initial discount for each recipient. This discount/contract combination creates artificial switching costs that otherwise would not exist. This is a typical arrangement in mobile phone or internet services markets, but also in many information markets. Information has high first copy costs, but lower marginal costs. With that cost structure, it is profitable to attract new cus-

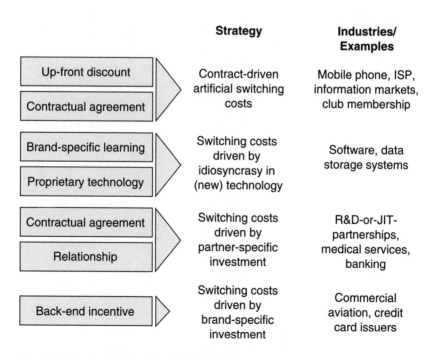

	Strategy	Industries/ Examples
Up-front discount / Contractual agreement	Contract-driven artificial switching costs	Mobile phone, ISP, information markets, club membership
Brand-specific learning / Proprietary technology	Switching costs driven by idiosyncrasy in (new) technology	Software, data storage systems
Contractual agreement / Relationship	Switching costs driven by partner-specific investment	R&D-or-JIT-partnerships, medical services, banking
Back-end incentive	Switching costs driven by brand-specific investment	Commercial aviation, credit card issuers

Figure 12-1: Switching Cost Strategies

tomers via (high) front-end discounts, but also paramount to insure a constant stream of revenues by contract to cover fixed costs. With that arrangement, customers become club members.

Brand-specific learning is often linked to new technology that has strong idiosyncratic features. Such features require brand-specific customer learning which, in turn, creates switching costs. We find this very often in the software or data storage industry. As markets mature, the potential for switching costs often diminishes. Customers accumulate knowledge which allows them to switch more freely and with fewer costs, as products become more standardized. The loyalty effect is temporary and closely linked to cycles of technological innovation: with a disruptive innovation, a new potential for idiosyncrasy-driven switching arises.

Just-in-time delivery systems are good examples for B2B arrangements in which switching costs result from a combination of contracts (which bind partners for some time) and personal relationships. Partner-specific investments drive this customer loyalty strategy. As both partners invest io the other, both are stuck with each other. Because the contract cannot cover all possible risks, strong personal relationships are needed to "fill in cracks left by more formal contractual and ownership structures."[1]

Frequent-flyer programs work in a similar way. The difference is that they are typically one-sided investments: the customer invests in the brand by accumulating purchasing volume. This strategy needs no formal safeguards or binding contracts. It is sufficient for the customer to accept the terms of the loyalty program. All the vendor needs is the ability to verify customer claims for incentives by controlling individual purchasing volume.

---

1 From: S.J. Carson, T.M. Devinney, G.R. Dowling and G. John: Understanding Institutional Designs within Marketing Value Systems, Journal of Marketing, 63, special issue 1999, 115–130.

PART 4

Mastering Customer Lock-in: Developing a Switching Cost-based Strategy

Part 4 is concerned with the implications of switching costs for business strategy. Switching cost affects a host of issues in strategy development and implementation that will be addressed in this section. Discussion proceeds in four steps:

First, we will look at how to develop strategy targeted at the customer base, non-brand users, and new buyers. An important issue is how to unfreeze entrenched users of competitive brands, and how to refreeze them through lock-in.

The second step is dedicated to the implementation of a strategy based on customer switching costs. This refers to:

- *developing the instruments necessary to monitor the success of a customer lock-in strategy. This includes the monitoring of the resulting change of customer equity and*
- *preparing the organization and implementing the changes necessary throughout the value chain.*

In a third step, we will look at how to monitor the contribution of your switching cost strategy to customer equity. The customer equity concept provides very valuable insight into the success of your strategy. The last step deals with the challenges of implementing a switching cost strategy in an organization.

Throughout part 4, the implications of switching costs for strategy development are discussed at the business division level, not the corporate level. Switching costs directly affect buyers and the interaction between competitors. It is at this level that the impact of lock-in on strategy is pervasive.

13

Differentiating the Strategy

The ultimate goal of management is to increase the profitability of a business. Rivalry in an industry is an important driver of company profits. But so are the distinctive competencies and capabilities of a company, its strategic resources. Modern strategic management is very much concerned with the management of such resources. It is targeted at developing and enhancing the competencies and capabilities within the company that are:

- valuable in the marketplace—because they eventually translate into a quality and/or cost advantage,
- rare—because no or only few other companies have them,
- costly for competitors to imitate—their price is high and/or it takes a long time to learn and integrate the capabilities,
- non-substitutable by other resources—no other capability serves the same purpose.

If a company's resources are all of that, that company has a distinct resource advantage over its competitors, forming the basis for a sustained competitive advantage and superior profitability.

This framework explains why some companies are more profitable than others within the same industry. It has been successfully applied in many cases and is an excellent complement to Porter's 5 forces industry analysis, which looks at the determinants of profits at the industry level.

Dell Computers is a good case for a resource-based analysis.[1] Dell has been outperforming all other computer hardware manufacturers over the last ten years. Its ROI is several times higher than industry average. This superior performance is based upon several resource advantages:

- Dell has perfected JIT purchasing of components such as hard drives or motherboards and orders most of them

---

1 This example is taken from: J. Barney (2001): Gaining and Sustaining Competitive Advantage, Prentice Hall.

after having sold a PC to a customer. Not only does that fast-forward revenues (Dell gets paid well before component costs are incurred), it prevents Dell from stocking hardware supplies over weeks that decline rapidly in value. (Consider that hardware components such as drives or motherboards decline 1–2% per week in value.)

- Dell operations are very sophisticated and completely integrated into the information flow across the whole value chain. Components which need no manipulation by Dell (monitors, displays) are delivered from suppliers directly to the customer. There is no reason to run them through a Dell warehouse. As Michael Dell once said: "We do not get our jollies from moving monitors around." Seemingly, others do.

- The internet is Dell's primary sales and service channel which integrates customer data into the work flow. Dell keeps the retailing margin and is faster.

The "Dell model" is widely known in the industry and even documented in a comprehensive HBS case study.[2] Why doesn't anybody copy this model? The answer is simple: The larger competitors (HP, IBM, and so on) are heavily locked-in to their sales channels. They could open an internet sales channel and some even did so. But they never committed themselves to Dell's approach. They were never ready to completely abandon their established sales channels through retailers. Their retaliation would have been fierce. HP and others would have lost most of their revenues through these channels and, for them, the internet was too small to compensate for that.

In the meantime, Dell perfected its model and in terms of strategic resources is now so far ahead that its only danger comes from industry factors.

Developing a strategy on the basis of switching costs requires a clear understanding of how this approach relates to the resource-based view of the firm. Customer lock-in is a goal to achieve. Strategy is concerned with the question of how to achieve it. Strategy development must address the issue of which resources are needed to successfully implement that strategy.

---

2 HBS case number 9-799-158, title: "Matching Dell." Order at: http://harvardbusinessonline.hbsp.harvard.edu/b02/en/common/item_detail.jhtml?id=799158.

ROLE OF CUSTOMER LOCK-IN
IN BUSINESS STRATEGY

Superior performance stems from being able to generate the greatest difference between the value provided to the customer and the costs incurred when creating that value. This implies that there are two principle ways of obtaining competitive advantage.

- Cost leadership: incur the lowest cost in creating a given value provided to the customer and sustain that cost position.
- Differentiation: provide the highest value to the customer at given costs.

The strategy of cost leadership is heavily dependent upon production volume.[3] Higher production volume drives average unit costs down—this is the well-known economies of scale phenomenon. However, some firms had to learn that selling more units may require an increasing number of product variations, creating complexity costs that offset the lower production costs per unit.

Until you reach that point, volume is the main driver of average costs. This is especially true in industries with high first-copy costs and high production fixed costs. It costs a lot to develop and promote a new software or movie, and second-copy costs are almost zero. Aircraft manufacturing is similar, for example, Airbus estimates the new "super jumbo" A380 to cost $20b in development. If they sell 100 pieces, that makes $200m per unit. If they sell 1,000, it's a tenth of that. Rumor has it that Airbus has sold the first A380s for less than $150m, far below the list price of $220–$230m. In such industries, volume is key.

Cost (and volume) leadership can be obtained if high demand customers are locked-in over an extended period of time, providing the necessary production volume for cost advantage. In the case of Airbus, this would mean to lock-in the large transcontinental Airlines (UA, Lufthansa, BA, and so on) with their demand for supersized airplanes. In general, it would mean to lock-in the majority of customers at the beginning of the product life cycle and then use the sustainable superior cost position to fend off competitors.

Product differentiation relies upon providing a superior value to customers. Note that a performance advantage follows only if

---

3 There are other factors that influence cost position. Among them are an exclusive, superior production, an operations technology, and exclusive access to low-cost suppliers. Also, a firm influences its cost position by choosing a certain number of product varieties and deciding upon product quality. Both factors drive costs up.

superior customer value translates into a price premium larger than the higher costs of providing more value. The magnitude of the price premium is proportional to the customer's perception of how much more value is offered. In general, customers pay more if the product or service is more suited to their individual needs.

With switching costs, this simple logic becomes more complicated because value is affected by the risk imposed on customers through lock-in. Before lock-in, rational customers will look at a brand's performance including insurance offered by the vendor. After entrenchment, a brand's performance disadvantage must be lower than the switching costs to prevent a customer to defect. Again, we must differentiate between buyers without switching costs on one side and the customer base on the other side.

In pure economic theory, the additional profit from customer lock-in comes from temporal price discrimination. Companies raise prices after customers are locked-in. Consider an example in which consumers can choose between two brands, A and B. Choosing either one leads to lock-in. This means that when they buy again (after one period in this example), they must buy the same brand again. Assume that customers have willingness-to-pay of $10 for brand A and $8 for brand B. Users of brand A have switching costs of $4. This implies that you can raise the price of brand A to $14 after lock-in: the price differential between A and B increases exactly by the height of the switching costs. In other words, beyond the value of the performance advantage, companies can command a price premium over the competitive brand up to users' switching costs.

In reality, this rather simple approach is very difficult to implement for several reasons:

- As we have discussed, rational customers will anticipate the second-period price increase of $4 and will demand a price of $6 in the first period or insurance at a value of $4 as compensation. This is the zero sum game: the average price over both periods is $10 ([$6+$14]/2). Alternatively, you charge a total of $24 ($10 in first, $14 in second period), but have additional costs for providing insurance of $4. In both cases, there is no additional profit from switching costs.
- With the latter model, you need to find a way to identify repeat buyers and charge them $14 instead of $10. It is not known that they are repeat buyers! In that case, your total profits might be reduced by $4 per unit.
- If customers are "myopic" and don't anticipate the price increase, they will feel unfairly treated and will try to damage

your company's reputation. This may lead to a negative sum game as you lose business with other customers.

This leads to the conclusion that finding a strategy to implement effective price discrimination against entrenched users is not as simple as economic theory suggests.

STRATEGY FOR YOUR CUSTOMER BASE

A customer base has invested specifically into a company's brand, for example, by accumulating brand-specific knowledge or bonus points as part of a back-end discount program. It experiences some degree of lock-in with this brand.

In a market with switching costs, the customer base is the most important asset. Not only is this the main source of revenues, it is crucial for developing a good reputation that motivates new buyers to adopt this brand and users of other brands to switch.

A good strategy for this segment consists of the following elements:

1. Building reputation. This means to consistently deliver superior quality and not to engage in opportunistic price increases for entrenched users. Inevitably, this kind of price discrimination will hurt one's chances to enlarge the customer base.
2. Deepen users' lock-in. Provide high-quality upgrades and value-enhancing complements so that users can leverage their brand-specific investment. The more they can use it, the better that investment was.
3. Focus on cross-selling and not on temporal price discrimination. Develop value-enhancing complements and also motivate partners to enlarge a particular brand. These enlargements are the basis for profitable price discrimination.

Profiting from customer lock-in means to gradually increase switching costs with a stream of valuable, but high-priced, complements. The game begins and does not end after a customer base has been established. If customers are milked, a company will run into severe problems.

Building Reputation

A good reputation is the cornerstone of the best strategy in a market with switching costs. Rational ("non-myopic") customers will—

all other things being equal—prefer the less risky vendor. All competitors will provide some insurance against lock-in risk, but complete insurance is unfeasible. Therefore, a good reputation will greatly enhance the chances to attract new buyers and switchers.

The alternative is to just milk the existing customer base by cutting quality and R&D to save costs. Deliver mediocre updates and complements—if at all—and extract whatever profits are possible from locked-in users.

This may be a very profitable short-term strategy, but it is a sure route to long term fiasco. First, milking will deter any potential user to join the current customer base. Excessive milking will not go undetected. Second, the customer base will shrink with users coming to the end of the usage cycle. Unsatisfied and exploited customers are almost certain to switch brands. Wouldn't you?

Reputation is a customer equity driver. It reduces the churn rate of your customer base and your chances to enlarge it. How does a company develop a good reputation? Good reputation results from continuously fulfilling quality promises. It is a signal that this supplier will deliver the promised quality after the contract is signed.[4] For reputation to develop, customers need to form networks in which they exchange their experience with a certain supplier.[5]

As with every communication process, the building of reputation is not perfect:

- It is affected by time lags. The longer it takes for customer experience to be spread, the lower are quality levels.[6]
- It is subject to individual perception. Other customers may or may not sanction a vendor because of bad word-of-mouth.[7] They may dispute the relevance of it or the originator's nobility.
- Not every quality deficiency is detected and communicated.
- Geographic distance and the degree of diversification influences the probability of negative experience reports reaching other customers.[8]

Most customers are aware of these imperfections, so vendors should help their customers to communicate their experience

---

4 See Herbig, Milewicz and Golden, 1994.
5 See Fombrun/Shanley 1990, Yoon/Guffey/Kijewski 1993.
6 See Shapiro 1982.
7 See Weigelt/Camerer 1988.
8 See Rao, Qu, and Ruekert 1999, p. 260.

with a brand, even if it is negative. Think of Cisco or other software companies operating bug bulletins. Is that risky? Yes. But this approach shifts the risk from customers to the supplier and that is what they want. They want to see that the vendor has a permanent incentive to deliver on his promises.

Building a good reputation takes time. Destroying it takes less. The more companies help to increase the efficiency of the process, the faster they will benefit from it.

Recent research on the process of reputation building suggests that different activities for reputation building exist.[9]

- symbolic actions by which companies communicate their identity with whatever means of formal communication
- competitive actions by which companies signal how they wish to compete with our companies (for example, their aggressiveness)
- relational actions which relate to any activities by which companies try to motivate customers and other stakeholders to engage in repeated transactions with them

This model provides good insight into the process of reputation building in markets with switching costs (see Table 13-1).

Symbolic actions include whether and how you communicate how important customers' brand-specific investment is to a company. Customers will feel more secure if they are provided with the highest return on their switching costs. For that, keeping promises must become a core element of the company image. Support the emergence of a community spirit among customers and offer a platform for their communication. All that signals commitment to customers who lock-in to a brand.

Relational actions refer to any one-on-one exchange between company and customers. Make it easy for customers to initiate meaningful exchange and control for their perceived value of this exchange. It takes many positive exchanges to build a lasting and good impression; it may take only one to destroy a good reputation.

With regard to competitive position, it is paramount to commit yourself to never letting competitors make your brand obsolete through innovation. Technological innovation can induce users to abandon their current brand early. Don't let that happen.

---

9 See: V.P. Rindova, S. Kotha (1999): Building reputation on the internet: lessons from Amazon.com and its competitors, working paper, University of Washington, available at: http://us.badm.washington.edu/kotha/personal/pdf%20files/amr_final.PDF.

Table 13-1: Building Reputation

Symbolic actions	• commitment to ongoing value enhancement of customers' brand-specific investment ("highest ROI on switching costs") • "promises kept"—a core element of company image • operating efficient communication platform for customers ("open source") • building a sense of community among customers
Competitive actions	• commitment to R&D: "never obsolete" • superiority in value
Relational actions	• emphasizing the building of relationships to customers • offering open communication channels • valuing input and motivating information exchange

If a customer feels no commitment to staying up-to-date, they will go elsewhere. Never think that price can compensate for being behind. This is not what customers want to hear when they are about to commit for years to a brand. They want to know that they have enough time to earn a decent return on their brand-specific investment.

Deepen Customer Lock-in

Put yourself in your customer's shoes. When does her brand-specific investment pay the highest dividends? The longer and more broadly she can use it profitably, then, her *return on switching costs* is the highest.

With a frequent-flyer program, that would mean the customer can use her miles on more routes, at more times, with more flexibility and less restrictions. Or she can purchase a wide variety of goods and services with them. With brand-specific learning, it means that this knowledge can be leveraged across a wider range of applications and the customer can put the knowledge to a more profitable use. With the technological lock-in of a system's architecture, it means that more complements for that system exist that give the user more flexibility in adapting it to his specific needs and enlarging it as he goes.

Look at this simple logic from the vendor's perspective and find how to deepen customers' lock-in by continuously providing upgrades and complements to your brand or technology that provide more opportunities for customers to profit from their brand-specific investment.

This approach benefits both sides. A nice example is Airbus. Airbus was the first producer of commercial aircraft to implement digital cockpit technology into its commercial airplanes (for example, fly-by-wire). Airbus now uses that technology across its whole range of aircraft, from the 100-seater A318 to the upcoming 600+-seater A380. It calls the "Flight Operational Commonality." Flight decks are virtually identical. Airbus claims that, as a result, training time for certification of pilots is significantly lower. Pilots can adapt to different Airbus airplanes faster once they are trained on an Airbus type.[10] Some types (A300 and A310) even have the same type rating, reducing certification time to a single day. It also reduces spare parts inventory and simplifies maintenance procedures.

This does a lot for airlines to commit to Airbus as the exclusive supplier of aircraft. What is required so be successful with that strategy? Provide upgrades and complements to a brand.

(1) UPGRADES   Rule #1: provide timely upgrades. Focus R&D effort on keeping technology up-to-date. Customers shouldn't find out that a company is not up to speed with the next "Y2K" problem. Timely and high quality upgrades lengthen the repurchasing cycle and produce a gradual lock-in effect. With every upgrade, customers will accept a limited (but positive) amount of additional brand-specific learning that comes with a more powerful solution. Thus, with every upgrade, customer lock-in becomes deeper and brand switch moves further away. Use this principle by providing value-enhancing upgrades that add new idiosyncrasies to the brand or technology.

At the same time, be reluctant with price discrimination via updates. Charging entrenched users excessively more for upgrades than new buyers would present a severe source of dissatisfaction and may damage your reputation. A better way to extract willingness-to-pay is to use complements.

(2) COMPLEMENTS   Rule #2: provide a stream of complements that add to the perceived value of the brand. Complements are additional applications for the brand-specific knowledge a customer acquires.

Airlines have been introducing many additional sources for acquiring and spending brand-specific frequent traveler miles. At Lufthansa, a traveler can acquire bonus miles by renting cars, buying an expensive Bang & Olufsen home stereo system, or using a cell phone. Bonus miles can be spent by air travel, ordering vintage

---

10 Source: http://www.airbus.com/media/commonality.asp#crosscrew.

wine, or giving a hot air balloon ride to someone. Lufthansa customers are not restricted to use their bonus miles only for air travel.

This complements the acquisition and use of frequent traveler miles without making them any less brand-specific. The same principle applies to learning the idiosyncrasies of an operating software or a site-specific investment by an industrial supplier. The more it can be put to profitable use, the better it is. In the case of Faurecia, Audi's seat supplier, delivering other components besides seats to Audi would complement the site-specific investment at Neuburg, Germany. Faurecia is a producer of a wide range of products, including acoustic packages, front ends, or cockpit modules. Extending the range of supplies delivered to Audi would complement the site-specific investment at Neuburg and accelerate earning a proper return on switching costs.

In many industries, complements to a certain technology come from different vendors forming value networks. Behind that option lies a crucial strategic choice. Do you license your brand or technology to partners and let them develop complements or are you going it alone? To make that decision, you need answers to the following questions:

1. Which complements will be valued by customers? Do they want them from a single source?
2. Will the technological underpinnings of these complements coincide with a company's core competencies?
3. Is a company's financial power sufficient to sustain the development of these complements? Of all or which?
4. What is the time-to-market for both options? Is time-to-market critical?
5. Is it a goal to move into the "complement arena"? What rivalry can be expected in these arenas and, consequently, what profit potential?

These questions should help to make a conscious and profit-enhancing strategic choice. In general, develop those complements that are critical for customers and for which exists the technological competence. Use competent partners in the development process if time-to-market is critical and the appropriate knowledge is lacking. Maintain sole ownership (production, distribution) if that complement is critical to a brand's success. Partner for the development and production of those complements that lie beyond your competence and/or are less valuable. Don't dismiss partnering as an option. There are many cases in which partnering proved to be very successful even for "big players" (for example, SAP, Microsoft).

Set Your Sights on Cross-selling

(1) SELLING PROPOSITION FOR COMPLEMENTS Complements are the basis for cross-selling. With switching costs, complements are where the profits lie. Now, everybody wants to cross-sell these days. What is so special about it in markets with switching costs? The difference lies with the selling proposition.

Take a look at Amazon.com. Amazon is a very successful cross-seller. Customers visiting Amazon's website and looking at a certain book will get recommendations for bundling their purchase with other items. Recommendations may be of related content and the bundle attractively priced *("best value")*. Also, Amazon presents bundles popular with other customers *("customers who bought this book also bought . . .")*. Other companies try to mimic this approach by implementing sophisticated CRM technology to find out which combination was bought in a bundle.

But with this and many other attempts at cross-selling, a value proposition is virtually non-existent. Even Amazon.com knows little about *why* a customer bought a particular bundle. There is no way to determine from only the sales history of a customer which books, bought at different points in time, served as complements.

So even with CRM, this type of cross-selling strategy is rarely a good approach. If you suggest or offer a lot, you hit something. But this is not very efficient. And if it is done too much, customers get angry at the hard sell.

> BMW in Germany does it a little bit more sophisticated. BMW requires all independent BMW dealers to pass on information on new car buyers. BMW stores this data along with the service history of the car and uses it to actively contact BMW drivers to cross-sell items related to their car. Assume that somebody bought a new 5-series BMW in July. BMW knows that this person owned a 3-series BMW before. In October, BMW will send out an email to this person promoting its offer of certified winter tires and snow chains. Both are not upward compatible so that the person has to buy new tires and chains. If BMW knows that the customer likes to ski, it will send a offer of a ski rack and so on. Attempts at cross-selling are made on the basis of individual customer profiles.

Brand-specific investment makes cross-selling simple. Often, it is easy to tell exactly which solutions will complement a brand or technology. Complementary products or service let customers leverage their brand-specific investment and put it to profitable use in additional applications. Look at what leverages that invest-ment—*this* is your selling proposition. It is one the customer will understand and value.

(2) PRICING COMPLEMENTS WITH SWITCHING COSTS   The cross-selling of complements to an idiosyncratic brand presents an enormous profit potential. Most of the profitable price discrimi-nation happens here. The HP printer case (discussed in part 1) underscores that point. How far can it go?

Let's expand the example used at the beginning of this chap-ter. The initial price of brand A was $10 and $8 for brand B. Switching costs of A-users amount to $4. Let's assume that the sup-plier of brand A introduces a complement, CA, that provides an additional value of $10 to the user (or sustaining the original value of $10) without requiring additional brand-specific invest-ment. What can be charged for CA?

Assume that B offers B plus CB (a comparable complement of comparable value) and charges $18 for the B/CB bundle. Thus, switching would cost A-users $22 ($18 plus switching costs of $4). This leads to CA being priced at $22 to extract the total willingness-to-pay from A-users. This solution requires CB and CA to be incompatible.

You think that $22 for the complement is unrealistically high? Think about the HP printer case. What happens when you run out of ink? You can buy a new set of HP printer cartridges at $60–$80 a set. Otherwise you need to buy a new printer. This would cost $50–$100 including the cartridges.[11] HP prices the car-tridge set square in the middle of the total switching costs spec-trum. The set is therefore very expensive (consider that about 50% goes to the retailer), but this is still better than buying a new printer.

A price premium that amounts to total customer switching costs can be commanded over the competitive brand. With com-plements in use, switching costs increase as other costly brand ele-ments are replaced when customers actually switch. Additional brand learning with complements (gradual lock-in) adds to that.

This solution does not change with a stream of consecutive complements. Companies can always charge the total switching

---

11 For the sake of simplicity, it has not been noted that the cartridges of a new printer (HP or otherwise) are typically not full. This vendor practice has been disputed in U.S. courts which ruled it legal. Therefore, to be exact you need to add the cost of the miss-ing ink in a new printer's cartridge.

costs. The only difference is to decide when to charge what increments of the total switching costs over time.

This example provides an idea how far this can go. How far a particular company should go is a matter of market reaction. HP can actually price cartridge sets so high because all vendors practice the same "high extraction" strategy for complements and many buyers are unaware of lock-in or dismiss it as irrelevant (they can't escape). This lack of competitiveness creates the excessive use of the price potential for complements.

If some vendors would price complements much lower, customers would be encouraged to switch brands. An industry-wide price reduction would follow. If consumers' outlook would be more far-reaching and if they would choose printers not on the basis of their initial price but their life-cycle costs, this process could be quite fast.

Another important issue to keep in mind is that the price premium increases with a perceived performance advantage of brand A over B (including complements). In competitive markets, companies need the performance advantage to sustain a high-extraction pricing for complements. The more different offerings are, the less customers will be concerned with the prices of complements.

The price premium commanded for performance advantages and switching costs work synergistically. If there is no performance advantage and the market is very competitive, there is little chance to extract switching costs through prices for complements. But if more value is offered, this also creates price potential for complements once customers are locked-in.

Profitable cross-selling requires you to keep ownership of those complements that you think are critical. In turn, this places a restriction on opening a "system" to other vendors. Otherwise, the profits go elsewhere. Companies need to be prepared for cross-selling within their organization. If the sales function is set up across product lines, it is difficult to sell bundles. In chapter 14 we will discuss pricing in more detail.

STRATEGY FOR ENTRENCHED USERS

Entrenched users experience switching costs when switching away from competitive brands. This is often the largest segment in mature industries, where adoption is high and the bulk of the business comes from repeat purchases. In order to motivate entrenched users to switch, companies must do the following:

- unfreeze them—initiate a decision process in which users evaluate the continuous use of their brand against competitive offerings
- move them—initiate the actual brand switch
- refreeze them—initiate brand lock-in

Unfreeze Entrenched Users

Unfreezing entrenched users means motivating them to seriously consider switching their brand or technology. Companies need to initiate a decision process in which users evaluate the continued use of their brand against competitive offerings. Some users may perform such an evaluation periodically, others start it only when severe dissatisfaction arises. Active marketers prefer not to wait for that. This raises the question of how the consideration to switch can be actively triggered. Entrenched users will consider switching when their value perception of their own brand or that of other brands changes. The more attractive an outside option becomes, the more positive is the outlook of switching.

Consider the customers of Baan, the Dutch business software company (www.baan.com) and subsidiary of SSA Global technologies. Founded in 1978 and an industry leader in the ERP software industry in the 1980s, Baan began to fall behind SAP and Oracle in the 1990s. Baan has been in troubled waters since then, reflected by many changes in ownership and management. Nevertheless, Baan has the image of being an industry visionary and committed to innovation.

Baan claims that its enterprise software "iBaan" is in use at more than 15,000 customer sites. Customers at these sites have invested heavily into the specifics of Baan software and experience significant switching costs. What could motivate iBaan users to abandon much of their massive brand-specific investment in software implementation or employee training? Following are some examples.

- The perception that Baan will reduce or even discontinue its development effort rendering iBaan obsolete in the near future.
- Innovations by competitors such as SAP, Oracle or Peoplesoft promising a significant advantage in performance.

- A competitor developing a special interface between his software and that of iBaan, enabling a faster, smoother and less costly transition from iBaan to that brand.

Switching ERP software is very, very costly. It involves a much more elaborate and costly transition process than switching from Microsoft to Linux. Also, the value perception of iBaan users hasn't changed much and competitors did not come through with a breakthrough innovation. Neither did a competitor appear with an interface reducing switching costs. This is why even troubled Baan has seen very few customers defect.

The Baan case sheds light on the difficulty of unfreezing deeply entrenched users. The switch must promise a leap in performance proportional to the switching costs involved. It greatly helps if customer switching costs are reduced by facilitating the transition process. But if users are so deeply entrenched, as Baan or SAP customers are, it is very difficult to unfreeze them.

Move Entrenched Users

To actually move entrenched users requires offering a solution to their needs that features a performance advantage large enough to compensate for their switching costs and whose risk seems acceptable.

In management practice, a popular strategy to attract "first-time buyers" and motivate them to invest specifically into a brand is to offer first-period discounts. This can be a dangerous strategy. To make it work, companies need to do the following:

- ensure a stable revenue stream from each customer that is large enough to make a profit on all costs incurred in servicing the customer, including the discount
- be aware of the churn problem (attracting customers who don't stay long enough); be selective to whom discounts are offered
- watch out for negative interaction with loyalty programs— and don't create revolving door customers.

All this calls for being very selective with discounts. Also consider that for very deeply entrenched users, initially giving away products for free may not suffice, as the Star Office case shows. To cut average switching costs of Microsoft Office users ($1,750) by half, Star Office would have to give a license away for free *and* give the buyer $875 in cash. Try to explain that to a CEO.

This does not mean that discounts don't work to move entrenched users of other brands. It means that often they can't do the job alone. They can assist with other instruments if used properly and selectively.

There is no way around a strategy of providing superior customer value through innovation. But be aware that a brand must not only be better, it must be so much better that the performance advantage compensates for much of the switching costs which users of other brands have. The rest might be covered by discounts—if they can be limited to desired users only.

The innovation approach has the strong appeal that it eliminates the need to identify first-time buyers, critical when up-front discounts are used. What would happen in the game console industry if Nintendo would price a new console plus one or two games below the costs of the games alone? This would attract first-time buyers and users of other brands, but also many Nintendo users who want the additional games but have no need for the console. For those, the discount would be largely wasted.[12]

Instead, suppose Nintendo brings a revolutionary new game console to the market. Switching costs for users originate from how many games they have because each game is a complement to the console. Assume that old Nintendo games are upward compatible. But to make full use of the new technology, users need new games. This scenario is typical in the video game business.

Any buyer of a bundle of the new console and a new game is now effectively a switcher. He either switches from another brand or upgrades so much that the old games are of little use. Switchers *and* upgraders exchange an inferior technology with a lot of games a superior game technology with fewer games (because of the lower number of games initially available). Both have the same switching costs. The same effect occurs during brand-specific learning instead of entrenchment by complements. A revolutionary new technology from your supplier can also render your brand-specific expertise obsolete.

Brand switching or upgrading occurs when the perceived value of the new technology is so much higher that it surpasses the value of an older console with many (but outdated) games. Consequently, the degree of innovation largely decides how much switching will occur and why.

---

12 Of course, they buy additional complements and become more entrenched, but you pay too high a price for that.

An incremental improvement of a brand provides little incentive to entrenched users of other brands to switch. Bundling that with high discounts may only motivate an existing customer base to upgrade or add complements at low costs. In order to compensate high switching costs, excessive discounts need to be offered that have a significant negative interference with the customer base.

In contrast, a revolutionary new technology makes everybody a brand switcher. This is because upgrading involves significant adaptation and the devaluation of old investments. In that case, up-front discounts treat everybody the same.

If the "revolutionary" technology is chosen, not all users of a particular brand might upgrade. Some may continue to use their old technology, some may even switch to competitors. Instead of deepening the lock-in of the existing customer base, they are set free. This is one of the reasons why companies with an entrenched customer base are reluctant to innovative radically. They lose the lock-in of the customer base as they must upgrade and restart the entrenchment process.

To profit from radical innovation, a customer base must be small and the number of entrenched users of other brands high. A majority of both groups must perceive your a particular technology as superior and so valuable that even high switching costs are compensated.

Refreeze New Buyers

Refreezing new customers is identical to deepening the lock-in of your customer base. The idea is to offer timely upgrades and a portfolio of complements that let users leverage their brand-specific investment. The more you motivate new customers to deepen their lock-in with a brand, the less they are prone to switch.

Strategy for New Buyers

New buyers are first-time buyers with no switching costs. Targeting them can negatively affect the strategy for other market segments. Therefore, before starting to develop a strategy for the segment of new buyers, a company should look at the importance of this segment.

In mature industries, such as soft drinks and breakfast cereals, there are very few new buyers and the adoption rate is high. The adoption rate of a new technology, product or service is high if a large majority (60%–70%) of potential users has made at least one buying decision and adopted a certain brand. Adoption is low if the majority has not made any buying decision yet. Low adoption is typical for a young industry or a fairly new technology, for example, digital photography or multi-media messaging services.

Late adopters are typically very risk-averse. Early adopters are typically risk-takers. Early adopters perceive themselves as innovators and trend-setters, scanning the environment for new solutions. Late adopters want to see a new technology being brought to profitable use before considering to buy. This makes their buying behavior and underlying motives for brand-selection very different.

In a mature industry, the relatively few new buyers left are usually highly risk-averse. After all, they have not bought yet because they felt the risk was too large. To attract risk-averse buyers, companies need to reduce the risk associated with switching costs. We have discussed two ways to accomplish that, by offering insurance and reducing switching costs. The problem is that both strategies may reduce lock-in of a customer base if its members select options targeted at new buyers. This might translate into fewer upgrades and complements being sold to the customer base—a case of negative interference between strategies targeted at different segments.

Again, it is critical to be able to discriminate between different segments and prevent customers from one segment buying what is intended for others. For that, the ability to identify repeat buyers and new buyers is critical.

Sometimes identification can be easy. Repeat buyers buy only complements and upgrades, whereas first-time buyers buy bundles. As we have discussed, however, pricing can motivate repeat buyers to buy offers for new buyers or entrenched users of other brands. If there is a variety of different bundles and many promotional offers on complements and upgrades, it's very hard to tell which buyer belongs to which segment.

If negative interference between the segments is significant, think about how important the segment of new buyers is. How much profit can it possibly provide? Compare that to the lower profits coming from the existing customer base. If the segment of new buyers is small, and interference with the customer base is large, it is profitable not to target first-time buyers. Before first-time buyers are targeted, analyze the possible interference.

14

Converting Switching Costs into Price Premiums

Pricing is the Litmus test of strategy. With little intervention from other factors, it shows how loyal customers are to a brand. If customer loyalty is high, a price premium can be commanded. Otherwise, only what the second-best brand gets can be charged. If a price premium cannot be charged over direct competitors, marketing strategy has failed to create customer preference and brand-loyalty.

Ultimately, switching costs are about the ability to charge price premiums. Airlines have implemented frequent flyer programs to increase customer loyalty and to charge higher prices than otherwise possible. The American Airlines referred to in chapters 2 and 3 clearly makes that point. It all comes down to the question of to what degree can you transform customer switching costs into price premiums? How can you sustain that premium? Both issues are rather tricky.

Let us take a look at two examples of companies which convert switching costs into price premiums to different degrees.

TWO EXAMPLES

Consider the HP printer case in chapter 1. With inkjet printers and their proprietary supplies, high technological switching costs are involved. But how high are they and what percentage of that does HP extract by the pricing of supplies? This question is surprisingly easy to answer. Let us assume that a person buys a new HP 5150 inkjet printer. This model runs around $100 at www.amazon.com or www.staples.com. The buyer uses it until the first set of cartridges is depleted and a new set is needed.[1] This is

---

1 For simplicity, assume that a new printer comes with a full set of cartridges. Technically, this is not correct. The general conclusions of this example, however, are not hampered by this assumption.

when switching costs become relevant. At this point, there are two options. The first option is to go out and buy a new set of cartridges for about $55. The second option is to sell the empty printer and buy a new one including the cartridges. How much is a used printer worth? Without a set of cartridges, a new printer is worth $45 ($100–$55). For a used printer, it is worth less than that, maybe $25. Correspondingly, the switching costs with the second option are $75 ($100 for the new printer minus the resale value of $25).

Relate the switching costs to the price of a new set of cartridges and it can be seen that HP extracts 73% of customer switching costs by cartridge prices ($55–$75).[2] This is quite impressive, especially considering that HP does this every time supplies are purchased. Also keep in mind that a cartridge costs $4–$5 to produce. Theoretically, HP could charge more to buyers who buy their third or fourth set of cartridges. Their switching costs increase because the resale value of a used printer declines rapidly. This is the primary reason why supplies for out-of-production printers are so expensive. It is critical to stay short of actual switching costs because companies don't want users to switch away from their brand.

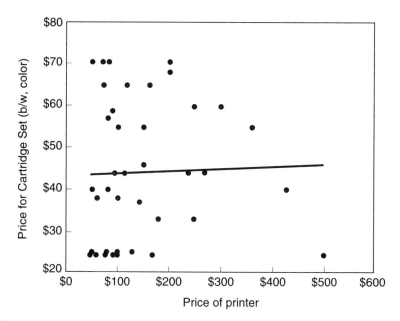

Figure 14-1: Printer Price versus Cartridges Costs

---

2 Both HP and the distributor do that.

Figure 14-1 shows how this practice of extracting a high share of switching costs is widespread. The graph plots the prices for 45 different color inkjet printer models from five brands (HP, Lexmark, Epson, Canon, and Dell) and the respective costs for a new set of cartridges. Prices were obtained from www.amazon.com, www.staples.com and www.dell.com. As you can see, for printers ranging from $50–$100, high extraction of switching costs is pervasive. Canon is a notable exception. Interestingly, for a broad price range ($50–$200), there is no significant difference in cartridge costs. Buying a more expensive printer does not make printing cheaper.

Learning costs are an essential element of switching costs. As the study by Gartner Group demonstrates, professional users of Microsoft Office invest heavily in this software, both on the individual and the organizational level. Migrating from Microsoft Office to Sun's Star Office costs $1,000 to $2,500 per user in a mid-sized company. Total switching costs comprise migration costs plus license costs for Star Office (about $35). But compared to switching costs, license costs are almost negligible. All this leads us to the conclusion that Microsoft extracts between 14% and 34% of professional user's switching costs ($350/$2,535 to $350/$1,035) via its pricing of new releases.

Why is this percentage so much lower than HP's? Is Microsoft's pricing less astute? The reason is that Microsoft operates in an environment where extraction of switching costs is not possible to the extent that it is done in HP's environment. There are different drivers at work that determine how much price discrimination is possible.

HOW MUCH PRICE DISCRIMINATION IS POSSIBLE?

In markets with switching costs, the only question that really matters is to what degree switching costs can be extracted via pricing. This is the most important driver of the profitability of a lock-in strategy. The examples presented here suggest that the following drivers are especially important:

- buying behavior
- new customer acquisition and critical mass effects
- pricing strategy of competitors and distributors
- standardization of interfaces
- reputational effects of excessive "milking"

Are Customers Myopic?

The HP example strongly suggests that in the printer industry excessive extraction of switching costs is possible because most buyers are myopic. They focus on the short-term costs of acquiring a printer but do not compare the life-cycle costs of various models. Estimating life-cycle costs would include the necessary number of cartridges over the expected life-span of the printer. But because customers are myopic, they get locked-in to a technology with high costs for supplies. Note that nobody is interested in creating transparency of life-cycle costs if customers don't care about it. Why should they? Cartridge suppliers and distributors both profit greatly from being able to charge a lot for supplies. As long as customers only look at printer prices, they are penalized for their negligence later on. This does not mean all buyers are myopic and can be charged more for supplies, complements, and new releases. It means that price premiums decrease when the time horizon of buyers purchasing decisions become longer.

Companies need to be aware of the way buyers make purchasing decisions. Assume that rationality in purchasing increases with the stakes. In B2B purchasing, where even small ticket items can create severe disruptions in production or logistics, elaborate supplier evaluations are performed to maximize the long-term value of supplier relationships. And similar to B2B, consumers will likely be more astute if the financial consequences of their decisions are greater. Maybe inkjet printers are just too cheap to spend a lot of time looking at life-cycle costs.

Very recently, HP announced its entry into the high-end copier business, attacking rivals such as Xerox and Minolta. According to a recent New York Times article, the new copier-based HP Laserjets 9055 and 9065, priced from $18,000 to $37,000, can print up to 85 pages a minute.[3] Companies in need of such high-performance printer/copier machines will surely look at relative long-term cost efficiency of competing brands including supplies and MSR. Very likely, contracts between HP dealers and customers will be long-term and will include prices for supplies and services. This transparency of follow-up costs will make the extraction of switching costs virtually impossible. In the European mobile phone service industry, the situation is similar. For a long time, service providers offered substantial discounts on new mobile phones to attract new customers and switchers. Dur-

---

3 Source: Steve Lohr (2003): Hewlett Now Wants to Be Your Copier Company, Too, New York Times (Internet Edition), November 17.

ing the late 1990s, rebates of $200+ were common. In turn, subscribers had to commit to a certain provider through a 12- to 24-month contractual agreement. But in this industry customers typically choose between brands on the basis of up-front discounts *and* prices for making calls. They are everything but myopic.

New Customer Acquisition and Network Effects

When buyers are myopic, there is room for extracting switching costs through the pricing of complements and new releases. But when they are not, excessive prices for supplies will severely limit a company's capability to attract new customers or keep them on board when they refresh. Look at the trade-off between extracting additional profits from an existing customer base and enlarging it. Larger players will make that decision different from smaller players. Larger players have less to win from enlarging their customer base. For them, it is more profitable to discriminate against their customer base and charge more for complements. One might think that this is what Microsoft is doing, but it's not. The example above shows that Microsoft only moderately extracts switching costs. If they could apply HP's approach, a single Office license would cost, on average, $1,300. This would almost quadruple its current list price of $350.

There are a number of reasons why this would be impossible. Switching costs vary greatly among Office users, depending on their level of entrenchment. In its above-mentioned study, Gartner Group acknowledges that switching costs ranging from $1,000 to $2,500 for professional users is a significant variance. For exclusive home users, switching costs can be significantly lower. What would happen if Microsoft starts to raise prices? Users at the lower end of the switching costs scale would start to switch brands as license fees exceed switching costs. Also consider that Office is a product with network externalities. Part of its value to an individual user comes from the total number of users. The more people use Office, the more files can be exchanged without compatibility problems. The same principle applies to fax machines, only to a greater extreme. If there is only one person on earth with a fax machine, it's worth nothing. If users at the lower end of the switching cost scale start to switch, this reduces the value of using Office for every other user. They become more inclined to switch and some will because of that reason and so forth. The result is a stampede of users switching brands once it has got rolling. A product such as Microsoft Office with strong network externalities is very vulnerable to reduction in its installed base, and Microsoft's ability to extract switching costs is limited. This is a good reason to stay away from HP's high extraction pricing.

Pricing Strategy of Competitors and Distributors

Most printer companies apply the same pricing strategy. They go in with low printer prices and charge a lot for cartridges. In fact, it matters little which brand is purchased. Distributors have little interest to reduce their margins on supplies because the effect on unit sales would be small. Once a printer is purchased it will need new cartridges, and they will be bought as long as it is cheaper than buying a new printer.

Obviously, the pricing strategy of competitors and distributors has a significant influence on complement pricing in markets with switching costs. When do suppliers have an incentive to deviate from a "high extraction" strategy? There is little incentive to do so if there is little or nothing to gain. Little is to gain if the revenues lost by cutting prices for cartridges are not compensated by additional revenues from new customers. In a saturated market in which many potential buyers own a printer, truly new customers are rare. Most buyers are replacing their outdated models.

Standardization of Interfaces

As noted before, standardization of technological interfaces between the components of a system eliminates lock-in. It is the only way to create competition among brands for follow-up purchases. Once a market is saturated, companies have no incentive to standardize. They would rather milk their customer base. However, in the early stages of market development, we might see companies collaborating and developing standards because it greatly enhances market size. This will happen if suppliers believe that many potential customers will not buy at all if they get locked-in. The standardization of interfaces eradicates any potential for price discrimination.

Spill-over of Excessive Milking

Printer manufacturers have done a great job of compartmentalizing their business. Few customers know that the printing division of HP is the single greatest profit maker in all of HP and that printer supplies play a significant part in that. In effect, HP and similar companies keep the possible customer dissatisfaction with excessive prices for supplies separate. It does not spill over to other businesses or divisions.

This must not be the case. Shocked by milking, customers may decide not to buy other products and services from that company. They may stick to HP cartridges until the printer is written off, but they will stop to consider buying, say, a notebook or a scanner from HP. A reputational spill-over of that kind can be disastrous to overall profits. It is important to note that reputational spill-over limits the potential to price discriminate against locked-in customers.

WHAT IS THE ESSENCE?

Companies cannot simply milk locked-in customers at will. But cases like HP or Microsoft also demonstrate that switching costs always provide some room for price discrimination and, therefore, additional profits. That potential for price premiums depends on several important drivers that should be observed. Of these factors, the ability to attract new customers and reputational spill-overs is the most important. These effects greatly influence your ability to grow. They need to be monitored closely to optimize pricing strategy.

15

Leveraging Customer Switching Costs through New Product Development

Customers are in a better position to use their brand-specific investment profitably if they can leverage this investment over a broad range of applications. That is the basic idea behind the strategy for the customer base discussed in chapter 13.

Software giant SAP has been very successful with this strategy. ERP software requires an extensive amount of brand-specific investment. With R/2, SAP was the first company to offer an integrated system of enterprise applications. SAP has systematically enlarged its portfolio of applications based on R/2 and R/3 over the last 20 years and now commands a dominating position in the ERP industry. Model train manufacturer Märklin (see www.marklin.com) applies the same approach. With its introduction of a digital multi-train control system, users were able operate up to 80 trains independently on the same layout. However, users need to invest heavily into the specifics of Märklin's digital control software. Therefore, Märklin is constantly enlarging digital applications to let customers leverage their switching costs.

A large customer base, locked-in by significant switching costs, is the most valuable asset of a company. Thus, commercialization of a new product must be primarily targeted at sustaining and increasing the value of that asset. Be aware of new product concepts that are targeted at new markets and divert a lot of resources from the customer base. From that perspective, Walter Hewlett has a point.

LOOKING AT THE PRODUCT DEVELOPMENT PROCESS

With customer lock-in, the new product development (NPD) strategy needs to be revised. Is a company's NPD targeted at developing value-enhancing upgrades and complements which actually allow customers to leverage their brand-specific investment? NPD consists of clearly defined stages and lock-in influences every one of them (see Figure 10.5).

During idea generation, it is paramount to employ a "leverage-based" approach and to look for what enhances customers' ability to leverage their investments that underlie lock-in. That can mean to extend the technological capabilities of a company, as the Märklin case demonstrates. For more than 140 years, Märklin has been a producer of model railroad hardware. Going digital means to go into software and understand the implications of that very different business for Märklin as well as brand users. What is required is the ability to translate customer needs into product attributes and engineering data in a way so that customers perceive lock-in as a necessary instrument to achieve superior value. The same principle applies to idea screening and concept testing.

As NPD gets closer to commercialization, it is important to focus business analysis on the contribution of new products and services to lock-in the customer base and the acquisition of new customers. Goals should be formulated accordingly. Note that the two goals can be conflicting. What deepens the lock-in of the established customer base can deter potential buyers from adopting the brand. The larger companies are, the more they will focus on the customer base.

What managers need to do is to forget thinking about a new product as something in its own right. The very idea of "leverage" is that upgrades, new complements, or applications enhance customer lock-in or make lock-in more attractive. Product testing should account for that. One aspect here is to test for the new product's "upgradeability." This refers to customers' judgment on how easy it is to transfer brand-specific investments into knowledge or infrastructure for an upgrade. The more difficult that is, the less will a new product support customer lock-in.

Commercialization can be supported by preannouncing. The availability of a new product is communicated before it is introduced to the market. A typical goal of that practice is to prepare customers and dealers for that move. In the realm of a switching cost strategy, it can be helpful to motivate customers to invest in a brand knowing that the necessary complements will be available shortly. Preannouncements, however, can only work if perceived as being credible by the target audience. Credibility can be a problem. For example, the software industry is notorious for

Table 15-1: Lock-in Strategy and the New Product Development Process

Stages in New Product Development	Influence of switching cost strategy
Idea generation (internal, external)	• importance of leverage-based approach
	• use lead user approach to find ideas for value-enhancing complements/upgrades
	• extend technological capabilities
Idea screening	• terminate "no-goes" early
	• importance of leverage-based criteria
Concept development and testing	• focus on target customers' perception of brand attractivity
Marketing strategy development	• formulate goals with respect to expected increase in brand-loyalty and new customer acquisition: share-of-wallet, extension of target market
Business analysis	• contribution of upgrade/complement to lock-in of customer base
	• contribution to acquisition of new buyers
Product development: prototype development and testing	• synergistic value, "upgradeability" • danger of losing sight of target ("product in its own right")
Test marketing	• simulation versus real life (standard, controlled)
	• rapid feedback
Commercialization	• preannouncing: lock-in before you go in
	• customer base comes first

overoptimistic or sometimes even misleading preannouncements ("vaporware"). Preannouncing works only if the target audience believes what it being promised and if it is backed up by action.

THE GOAL: PROGRESSIVE LOCK-IN OF CUSTOMERS

One of the key capabilities of companies pursuing a lock-in strategy is the ability to progressively lock-in customers. This means to motivate customers to adopt a brand and progressively increase their brand-specific investment over time. This is Airbus's strategy. Customers with all-Boeing fleets are offered substantial discounts to adopt Airbuses. Once customers have switched to a new Airbus type, adoption of the next Airbus type results in lower costs to certify pilots, lower costs of maintenance, and so on. It pays to move to an all-Airbus fleet over time, which makes the switch back to Boeing increasingly less likely. With this approach, lock-in increases gradually. It leaves customers the freedom to stop at any time along the way. Some airlines deliberately fly both Airbus and Boeing jets to become less entrenched. They forsake cost savings from homogeneous fleets to gain more power in buying negotiations and to buy jets cheaper.

Being able to progressively lock-in customers requires offering a portfolio of product and service options ranging from introductory offers attracting first-time buyers to highly entrenching products and complements for the advanced user who appreciates the added value they provide. Customers can follow a path that locks them in step-by-step. Of course, they can stop at each step, depending on their risk-taking behavior and the benefits they seek. However, it is the goal to move them as far as is possible and profitable. Developing such a portfolio of options involves distinctive capabilities:

- to identify the critical value propositions for different customer segments
- to introduce a complex mix of products and services with well-defined switching costs to the market
- to develop the necessary relationships with customers which are crucial to position the company as a trustworthy partner

eBay is a good example. The savviness of the millions of eBay users in designing auctions varies greatly. There are "powersellers" who have made auctioning their business and know every nook and cranny of eBay's idiosyncratic auction system. For them, an advanced set of eBay-specific tools to optimize auctions is offered (see http://pages.eBay.com/services/buyandsell/). But for the first-timer, it is fairly easy to set up an auction. This is where customer lock-in starts in this industry, at the very low end of the spectrum because so many potential eBay customers have little or no experience with internet-based auctions. As experience is gained, more time is invested in learning how to optimize an eBay auction, step-by-step and with increasing lock-in. At the same time, eBay clearly signals its solitary dedication to the operation of a global trading and auction platform. This secures the customer's investment in eBay-specific knowledge.

16

Dealer Support for Your Lock-in Strategy

Distribution strategy is a complex coordination issue involving a diverse range of tasks. The flow of goods and services over several levels of distribution needs to be efficiently managed. For that, relevant information must pass between the partners in a coherent and timely fashion. Often, distributors provide value-enhancing services to the customer for which they need the support of the supplier. Over the last ten years, more companies and their distribution partners have tried to convert their channels into what is called "value-enhancing networks." Institutions in these networks coordinate their activities across the channel to improve the performance of the entire chain. The egocentric perspective of trying to maximize profit on a single level is replaced by a holistic approach. Initially, this seemed a rather strange idea to many companies, as the past was often characterized by persistent channel conflict. But managers eventually realized that there is more to gain if channel members work in a concerted way. Consequently, arm's-length relationships to dealers have been replaced by long-term contracts and strategic alliances.

Channel strategy can be a powerful source of competitive advantage. For example, franchising is a superior model of channel design because it combines strong entrepreneurial incentives on the local business level with a powerful and integrated knowledge network. The rapid growth of many franchising systems shows that their capacity to learn and leverage management knowledge is much higher than that of conventional channel designs.

So, how can channel design help with a lock-in strategy? Here are some examples:

- providing additional sources of customer lock-in
- assembling complementary products from different suppliers strengthens the lock-in effect
- reducing customer uncertainty

PROVIDE ADDITIONAL SOURCES OF LOCK-IN

Caterpillar is famous for its strong ties to independent dealers. Dealers provide critical services to keep Caterpillar's machines working including storing spare parts and performing necessary repairs. They negotiate with customers and coordinate delivery. Caterpillar stresses the dealer's profitability and performance, provides extraordinary dealer support, and emphasizes full, honest, and frequent communication. This is because dealers are instrumental in creating customer lock-in. In the short term, customers may have to rely on the delivery of brand-specific spare parts. But the long-term relationship to the customer extending beyond the use of some of Caterpillar's equipment is created by the dealer. Accordingly, Caterpillar goes to great lengths in supporting dealers to establish a fruitful relationship to customers. This is a nice example of a company explicitly using channel partners to provide additional sources of lock-in. As discussed in chapter 11, switching costs can also be developed on the basis of value-adding personal relationships. We have called them emotional switching costs. With an indirect sales approach, rely on dealers to develop that bond.

If dealers are a critical source of customer lock-in, channel control becomes very important. Effective channel control rests upon a functioning strategic and operational co-alignment of activities at both levels of the channel. For that mutual commitment, trust and a contract serving as safeguard against abuse of the relationship is needed.

ASSORTMENT FUNCTION

Distributors are important because of their role in creating a meaningful assortment of products and services from various suppliers. When office supplies are needed it's nice to go to the nearest Staples and find everything in one stop. Dealers providing the right products and services can help create stronger customer lock-in to a particular brand. Sometimes customers are locked-in to a system of goods from different suppliers and not into a specific brand. This is when the dealer's assortment function becomes critical. For example, this is the case when the service provided by an independent dealer complements the hardware and creates additional switching costs. In a way, Caterpillar dealers are co-producers in creating lock-in because of the importance of the service they provide which, in turn, strengthens the relationship between the customer and Caterpillar. Microsoft is dependent upon many other software producers in creating lock-in to Windows. Because Windows-based software products for so many applications exist, Windows is an attractive operating system.

REDUCING CUSTOMER UNCERTAINTY

With switching costs, buyers face uncertainty because of the unknown consequences of lock-in. They will try to avoid lock-in traps. Therefore, dealers should help with suppliers' efforts to reduce the customer's uncertainty. As we discussed earlier, it is preferable to do that by offering insurance instead of cutting down on the amount of brand-specific investment. Keep in mind that customers contract with a dealer, not the actual manufacturer. It is this contract that may or may not provide insurance against exploitation of switching costs.

What can be learned is that channel design can be a source of competitive advantage. Considering that distribution channels are hard to change—the supplier himself is getting locked-in to long-term channel relationships and contracts—this advantage can be sustainable for quite some time. With an indirect sales approach, dealers can be helpful in supporting lock-in strategy. Actively engage dealers in a strategy that strengthens customer lock-in. Selecting and supporting dealers should be targeted at that goal. Among the many selection criteria used in management practice (size, sales performance, managerial capabilities, market coverage, and so on), the dealer's competence and motivation to provide additional sources of lock-in into a particular brand are crucial.

17

Addressing Customers' Risk in Communication

For buyers, locking into a certain brand is a trade-off between the brand's future performance and switching costs. Rational buyers will look for ways to reduce the risk involved. A company's communication should assist in risk-reduction efforts. Formal and informal communication to the target market should address the risk inherent in getting locked-in and offer information on why customers can rest assured when locking into a brand.

In general, brand communication is supposed to increase brand equity by creating brand awareness, creating the desired brand associations and improving perceived brand quality. These goals are instrumental in increasing profits by higher brand-loyalty or margins (see Figure 17-1).

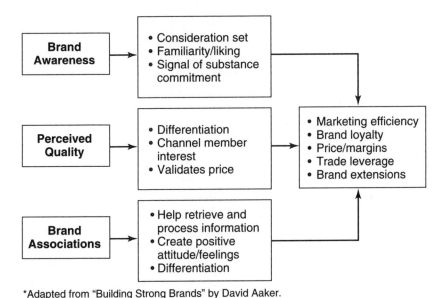

*Adapted from "Building Strong Brands" by David Aaker.

Figure 17-1: Brand Communication Process

Switching costs will likely change the relevance buyers place upon certain types of information. They will want to know about the risk of their investment into a brand. This assumes that buyers think about lock-in before they get engaged. The simple conclusion is that companies may need to address the risk issue and to do it the right way. Practice shows that options range from not addressing the risk issue at all to being very explicit about it.

HP, for example, does not address the concept of risk, but rather focuses on other product features such as print quality. When they introduced the HP 970C inkjet printer, the focus of the print campaign was solely on print quality.

The message is simple—With this printer, printouts become like reality. They are virtually indistinguishable from high-resolution pictures. But why doesn't HP address the lock-in problem? Perhaps it doesn't feel that it is relevant to buyers who concentrate on quality. HP may also think that addressing lock-in may confuse consumers unaware of impending lock-in and keep them from buying. The vast majority of printer buyers are not novices. Typically, they have owned several printers in the past and are well aware of the high costs of cartridges for whatever brand they own. The goal is to focus on superior quality to compensate for the high costs of printing. To achieve that purpose, the HP 970C campaign is very well-designed.

For IBM's e-business hosting services, Ogilvy developed a different approach. The agency described its task as follows: "The market not only didn't know IBM offered top-tier co-location web hosting services, but the offering itself had a commodity perception. Our techie target audience responds to image as much as competence. We needed to position IBM with a cutting edge flavor to put our brand on an even playing field with newer, smaller competitors."[1] One of the three print ads reads: "It's your web site. It's your e-Business. It's your server. It's our reputation."

Central to this print campaign is the significant risk that results from server downtime. In case of server failure, companies cannot change their hosting service on short notice. Downtime can quickly turn into revenue loss. IBM's answer is simple—since it is IBM's reputation that is on the line, it will do everything it can do to keep your business up and running. And that—presumably—is a lot. This is one of the cases in which companies offer their high reputation as insurance against the risk resulting from lock-in.

Computer Associates makes an even bolder reference to risk in its award-winning TV commercial "Amnesia." The spot features three managers on their way to a meeting. The two younger of the trio, and apparently those who have all the critical information, are knocked unconscious, one by running against an open file cabinet and one by knocking his head against the conference table. Finally, the senior and ill-informed manager of the three is left to his own devices facing a group of concerned business partners. Ad Age comments: "If accidents usually happen close to home, you ought to see the office. Assistants succumb to a series of consciousness-losing pratfalls in a spot for Computer Associates' Bright Stor storage software. In our data-driven meeting world, this commercial strongly asserts the importance of having backup."[1]

Why does HP downplay risk and IBM and CA put in the center of their message? When should you do that? It is necessary to be explicit if risk is relevant to customers. Lock-in is clearly relevant to customers of hosting services who integrate content management and databases into their websites. For such customers, it is reassuring to know that "Big Blue's" reputation is on the line. Computer Associates (CA) goes even further. CA puts a bright spotlight on a risk-related issue. What companies don't want, on the other hand, is getting customers so worried about risk that they choose a different brand or don't buy anymore. The lesson is that companies should address risk when relevant, but do it smartly. Offer concrete advice why switching costs are safe with your company.

---

1 Source: http://www.adage.com/images/random/best2003.pdf.

SUMMARY OF PART 4

An existing customer base is the most important asset, especially in a market with switching costs. Locked-in customers provide a stable revenue stream and increase chances to cross- and up-sell. However, lock-in does not imply that customers can be milked at will by simple price discrimination. Milking will eventually cause excessive switching and loss of reputation. This is a short-lived business model.

Enhance the value of customers' brand-specific investment by continuously providing additional applications that give customers enhanced opportunities to leverage the value of their switching costs. Both sides profit from that approach. Complements and value-enhancing new applications for brand-specific investment should form the basis for customer acquisition and retention strategy. Complements increase customer switching costs and provide ample opportunity to profitably price discriminate between the existing customer base and first-time buyers. In most cases, simple intertemporal price discrimination ("cheap today, expensive tomorrow") does not work.

Enlarging the existing customer base can hurt profits. The problem is that any strategy targeted at first-time buyers (entrenched users of other brands, new buyers) can severely hurt profits generated by the customer base. The use of up-front discounts is downright hazardous if companies cannot limit their availability to "real" first-time buyers. AOL is a case in point with its excessive use of up-front discounts that are used by large portions of their customer base.

Technological innovation is a better way to profit from switching costs, but it is not a sure bet either. Radical innovation can be necessary to generate the superior value needed to compensate for high switching costs of entrenched users of other brands. This may require upgraders from a customer base to abandon their brand-specific investment, making them "switchers," too. Thus, look carefully at how many members of a customer base intend to do that. If too many of them intend to "stay behind," the aggressive pursuit of first-time buyers can be highly unprofitable.

A strategy focused on customer lock-in implies new marketing priorities.

Product strategy is crucial to develop and sustain customer lock-in. It largely depends on the innovative capabilities of the company to create products and services that add value to the customer, but require brand-specific investment. The idea of progressive lock-in with ever deeper customer entrenchment and stronger brand-loyalty calls for the development of an array of options that customers go through step-by-step. Pricing can also be used as a lock-in instrument, but you should be aware of its pitfalls. Loyalty reward systems are rather difficult to manage and can easily end in a negative-sum game.

Communication is an important tool in markets with switching costs. Faced with impending lock-in, customers will be concerned with the safety of their brand-specific investment before they get entrenched: Can they expect a proper return on that investment? To address this concern is tricky. On the one hand, customers want an answer. On the other hand, you don't want to give too much attention to the issue of safety. It may raise hidden concerns. Here are some principles for your communication which balance both matters.

- Clearly explain to the customer the relationship between brand-specific investment and the added value it provides. Again, eBay is a case in point. Empirical research shows that auction prices correlate positively with a seller's reputation. There is a positive relationship between loyalty to eBay and the success of an auction. The more loyal users are, the higher the prices that can be achieved. It pays to learn the idiosyncrasies of this auction model; it pays to invest brand-specific.

- Develop a reputation as a reliable source of value-enhancing upgrades and complements that safeguard customers. Customers who invest brand-specific have a long-term view of things. Use satisfied customers as the primary source of communication. Provide them with a network to exchange their experiences and open this network to new customers.

Many companies in high-technology industries stress the superiority of their technology in their communication. This is not bad, but it does not address important concerns of customers faced with switching costs. How many related investments will follow? How long will the company be there to service and improve that technology? Is this the right partner for a long-term relationship? These questions are to be addressed in both formal and informal communication.

In distribution, motivate service and sales partners to develop value-enhancing complements to a certain brand. SAP has used this strategy in marketing its ERP software very successfully. When doing so, bind partners to companies via contracts that allow control over dealings with customers. It is very important to control the quality of services. Dell employs a direct sales approach and has integrated the distribution and service channel to give the most control possible. This is preferable when the quality of distribution and service and the efficiency of logistics are highly critical. Dell uses a segment of its web-based distribution channel—the "Premier Pages"—to create switching costs for larger customers. Dell explains: "Premier Page web sites are customized, password-protected extranet sites, which Dell creates for its corporate and public-sector customers. They provide one-stop access to simplified purchasing, purchase history reporting, order status and help desk support." Dell operates several thousand of these sites at www.dell.com. This is a nice example for creating switching costs by customizing the distribution function. For customers, switching to HP or IBM would result in substantial additional transaction costs.

PART 5

Closing the Loop

Where does a company stand with regard to their customer lock-in strategy? This is the starting point of part 5, the final section of this book. From a more generic view on strategic situation analysis, we will move on to a specific analysis of the contribution of customer lock-in to customer equity. The customer equity concept allows a very detailed analysis of the ability to extract profits from a customer base. Because of its superb ability to differentiate between customer acquisition and retention, it is very suitable to a switching cost-based strategy.

A customer lock-in strategy may also require changes to an organization. After all the hoopla about "total customer satisfaction," the idea of locking-in customers may sound quite strange to employees. Prepare for thoroughly explaining a new approach and also adapting the structure of the organization.

A crucial imperative is the ability to balance customer acquisition and retention. We will address that issue in more detail in chapter 19. A short outlook ends part 5.

18

Monitoring the Contribution of Customer Lock-in

WHERE DO YOU STAND?

Simple logic suggests that the long-term success of your business strategy depends on two variables:

- the degree of penetration of your target market
- the extent to which your customers experience switching costs

The more the target market is penetrated, the larger the market share. In fixed-cost intensive industries, this can be the foundation for a significant cost advantage. But high penetration does not necessarily mean that this advantage is sustainable. Sustainability depends on the ability to retain customers. This is where customer lock-in makes a difference. Customer switching costs increase the probability of a customer base being loyal and buying upgrades and complements. Customer switching costs determine the ability to generate a low-risk, stable revenue stream with greater margins due to price discrimination. Figure 18-1 summarizes the possible outcomes of a lock-in-based strategy using the two variables.

Achieving strong lock-in of the majority of the target market is an ideal position. Microsoft is such a key player in the office application software industry. SAP is to a lesser extent in the ERP software business. As a supplier, the focus is on preventing brand switching in that position and acquiring new buyers entering the market.

Insufficient lock-in calls for motivating customers to increase their brand-specific investment. In this situation, a company is not tapping the full potential of its extensive customer base. When moving from the upper right quadrant to the target position, expect to lose customers not willing to engage in higher switching costs. Such customers will defect. This is very much acceptable as long as more customer equity is added with those customers who

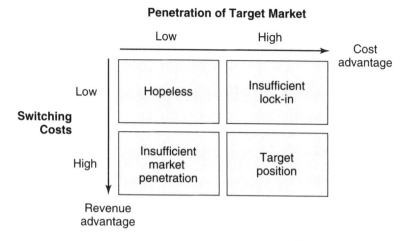

Figure 18-1: Strategy Output Matrix

stay on board than lost with those who defect. Somewhere along the way an optimum is reached. Customer equity losses from defecting customers who are unwilling to engage in higher switching costs equal the equity gains from higher lock-in of those that are loyal.

It seems that many successful consumer brands are in a position of insufficient lock-in. Think of Mercedes-Benz or BMW in Germany. They hold large market shares in the luxury car segment but depend on simple brand-loyalty to sustain it. "Hard" switching costs practically do not exist. Clearly, with increasing competition from new entrants, this is a precarious situation.

Insufficient penetration results from a product strategy that keeps risk-averse buyers from adopting a brand. If the customer base is small but highly entrenched, this strongly hints at your customers being willing to accept higher switching costs than other buyers. Reduce the risk of high switching costs for those buyers by diversifying the product portfolio. This position is very good in the "high value/high switching costs" market and not so good in the "medium value/medium switching costs" market. The key is to come up with a less-entrenching version of a particular brand and position it at a value level low enough to prevent cannibalization with the original version.

Smaller and highly innovative companies tend to end up in this situation. They focus their development effort on a few risk-prone customers willing to partner with them, leading to highly entrenching solutions of superb quality which fail to appeal to mainstream customers. A differentiated approach is necessary if such companies wish to extend their customer base.

A position in the upper left quadrant indicates neither success in penetrating your market nor the creation of significant switching costs. This qualifies as nothing but a complete failure of a lock-in strategy.

This model provides a sound framework for monitoring the success of a lock-in strategy. The measurement of customer equity drivers should be performed on a regular basis to provide quick feedback on a strategy's results.

CUSTOMER EQUITY IMPACT
OF CUSTOMER LOCK-IN

Lately, the idea of managing the customer base like a financial asset has become very popular. This is the principal idea of customer equity management. It looks at the revenue side of the profit equation and the direct costs of acquiring and retaining customers. Try to optimize the profit resulting from the acquisition and retention of a customer base.

With switching costs, this is no different. Look at different drivers of customer equity and be aware of the impact of customer lock-in on the value of this asset. This is the core idea of this chapter. But first, let us look at what customer equity management is about.

Principles of Customer Equity Management

Customer equity management is about properly monitoring and managing the revenue stream generated by a business unit's customer base. The goal is to extract maximum profit from the customer base over a certain time period.

To measure customer equity is not easy. It requires a model that captures the various variables of customer equity and their rather complex interaction. At the same time, it should be simple enough for implementation in everyday use. There are many customer equity models "in circulation" and they are quite impressive with their complex mathematical equations. But the following is key to understanding how to measure customer equity.

A service business was started on January 1, 2002. There is a market of 100,000 accessible and valuable customers out there for service. By December 31, 2002, 3,000 customers have been acquired who have made at least one purchase. This gives an acquisition rate of 3%, which is the first important driver of customer equity. This rate depends on the estimation of the number of target customers and the results of an acquisition strategy. The next important driver is the number of repeat customers. How many buy again? Repeat customers buy again to replace, upgrade or complement their initial purchase. Let's say 1,500 of the 3,000 customers have done so in 2003. Then, the retention rate is 50% in relation to the customer base by the end of 2002 or 1.5% in relation to the target market. Whether these are high or low numbers depends on the industry.

Acquisition and retention rates drive the equity of the customer base. This customer base consists of cohorts. A cohort is a set of retained customers acquired during a certain time period (in 2002, in this example). The idea of cohorts is important because the value of cohorts can be very different. The longer a customer stays with a certain supplier, the higher the value for the company. Often, "older" customers buy more and generate lower costs. Thus, customers from older cohorts can be more profitable than those from younger cohorts.

In markets with switching costs, supplier reputation is an important risk reducer for new customers. Reputation is developed by fulfilling promises to customers who share their experience with other buyers and prospects. Through this mechanism, the satisfaction of customers in older cohorts drives the acquisition rate in younger cohorts.

A graphical model of customer equity is shown in Figure 18.2.

Both acquisition and retention rate drive the number of units sold. Multiply this number with the gross margin (the difference between price and the costs of the goods sold [p – COGS]). For retained customers, differentiate between upgrades, new releases, and complements if their adoption rates, prices, and costs vary significantly.

Note that customer cohorts interact. One reason is the reputation building process. Another reason is the adoption of a new product or technology follows a well-defined process in which risk-takers buy first and risk-averse customers buy later. Risk-averse customers want to see the new technology "in action" and well-proved. For that, early buyers (risk-takers in early cohorts) are indispensable.

The concept of customer equity results in a number of important principles for the acquisition and retention of customers:[1]

---

[1] See: Blattberg, R.C., G. Getz and J.S. Thomas (2001): Customer Equity: Building and Managing Relationships as Valuable Assets, Harvard Business School Press.

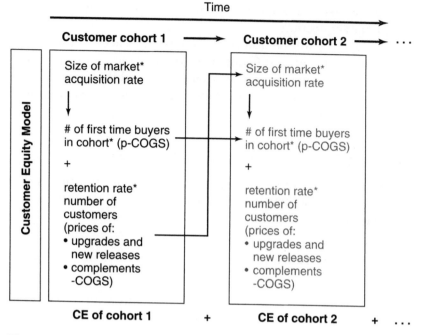

Figure 18-2: Customer Equity Model

1. Any marketing expenditure is an investment, be it targeted at new buyers or a customer base. This investment must pay off. For that it must result in a sufficiently large revenue stream from each customer.
2. Spend less on acquisition and retention if response rates are high, and vice versa.
3. Spend more on the acquisition of a customer if a higher future revenue stream can be expected (minus COGS and retention costs) from them, and vice versa.
4. Account for the risk when dependent on a future revenue stream. The later the acquisition or retention investment, can be recovered, the lower that investment should be.
5. Not every customer is worth retaining. If prices have to be cut for a high-value customer too much to keep them "on board," it is better to let them defect instead of charging lower prices to others who don't. To aim for zero defection is economic nonsense.
6. Even with high loyalty of your customers, you should never forget new customer acquisition. If 20% of your customers defect every year, the equity of your customer base is cut by

half in less than 2 years if you do not replenish it by new customer acquisition.[2]

7. Manage the interaction between customer acquisition and retention programs. Companies are likely to incur interaction when acquisition instruments are used that appeal to your customer base. Learn how to attract new buyers without creating revolving door customers.

Switching Costs and Customer Equity Drivers

Proper customer equity management requires monitoring its key drivers on an ongoing basis. This refers to the acquisition and retention rate.

ACQUISITION RATE DRIVERS Acquisition rate is driven by the following variables:

- Value advantage of a brand over competitive brands as perceived by potential customers
- Perceived risk in adopting a brand caused by subsequent switching costs
- Acquisition incentives (for example, up-front discounts) and insurance offered against lock-in

Prospective customers will look at the relative value of a brand and their risk position resulting from adopting it. The acquisition rate increases if relative brand value increases and risk decreases.

Switching costs will always lead to lower acquisition rates. But this is not necessarily bad. Remember, a larger customer base and a higher retention rate does not automatically create a more profitable customer base. Look at the profit that results from acquiring and retaining customers. Switching costs greatly enhance chances to cross-sell over a longer time period at higher prices. It does not hurt if switching costs are imposed on customers that lead to a smaller, but more profitable, customer base.

The acquisition rate can be too low. It is too low if enough customers can't be attracted with a high potential for profitable cross-selling, up-selling and upgrades. In that case, there is either a value or a risk problem. The value problem results from marketing a brand that—from the customer's view—is simply not

---

2 A defection rate of 20% and a discount rate of 10% devalue the revenues from your customer base by a combined 30% per year. With no new customer acquisition and constant prices, your customer base (100%) is worth $0.7^3 = 34.3\%$ after 3 years, or 49% (0.7^2) after 2 years.

competitive. The risk problem results from imposing excessive switching costs on customers. This makes a brand too risky to adopt. Either reduce the amount of brand-specific investment necessary or offer more insurance.

Don't be surprised when the adoption rate changes over time. There are two forces at work.

- When companies start building a customer base, they also start building a reputation. Reputation is critical to attract more risk-averse buyers. This is a force that leads the acquisition rate to increase.
- The first customers acquired are probably risk-takers. Later customers are more risk-averse. The chances of acquiring first-time buyers weaken if switching costs are not reduced. This is a factor that slows the acquisition rate down.

Overall, the acquisition rate should go down over time. It declines fast if high switching costs are imposed on your users, and higher-value customers are targeted first and lower-value customers later.

RETENTION RATE DRIVERS   Retention rate is driven by the following variables.

- customers' switching rate—these are customers who abandon one brand and adopt another
- the adoption rate of upgrades (including new releases) and complements
- a company's share in selling complements to their customer base

The adoption rate of upgrades and complements is a critical factor for customer equity. This rate shows the degree to which customers become entrenched in a certain brand. The more aggressively they update and enlarge the system, the higher is their lock-in. Customers "fall behind" if they stop upgrading and buying complements. Then, a brand switch becomes more likely. Thus, look closely at what acquired customers buy over time. It is important to monitor their degree of lock-in as it determines their probability to generate revenues in the future. It is not enough to simply register users as repeat buyers.

Look at a company's share in the selling of complements due to partner cooperation. A decreasing share in a customer's brand-related investment is a sign of partners gaining an advantage on the basis of a brand-specific investment of customers that you initiated. This is to be expected if you refrain from developing complements that many users need.

Be cautious in analyzing brand switching. Brand switching is necessary to rid the customer base of low-value customers attracted by excessive acquisition incentives. Minimize attracting this kind of customer but in practice you can't prevent it completely. This implies that some dropping out or switching should occur. However, it should not occur with high-value customers.

Measuring the Customer Equity Impact

As with every strategy, monitor the success of a strategy built on customer lock-in. Success in acquiring and retaining customers should be monitored on the following basis.

1. Look at the change of the acquisition rate over time and why it is changing. Differentiate value problems from risk problems and react accordingly. If the acquisition rate is higher than expected, the wrong type of customers may be attracted. Be prepared to fine-tune the acquisition approach as you learn how to attract actual members of target segments. With that, don't be afraid of trial and error.

2. It is extremely important to monitor the adoption of complements and upgrades by the brand users. This is what drives retention with switching costs. Are users strengthening their lock-in? If not, how effective is the product development strategy? Are users provided with valuable options—from their perspective—to leverage their brand-specific investment?

3. Are complements priced in a way that allows for effective price discrimination without damaging the value of the customer base? Remember, this is the primary source of profits from switching costs.

4. When are brand users considering switching brands? What initiates that consideration? Is it a standard repurchasing cycle or is it triggered by some critical event? How many entrenched customers prefer to bear the switching costs instead of sticking to you? Why do they do that? How valuable are defecting users?

There are clear signs of danger that every company should be aware of. One sign is a decreasing depth of brand entrenchment in your customer base which results from a lack of brand-specific investment. Don't simply measure brand adoption, but measure changes in brand entrenchment. Analyze the underlying reasons for insufficient entrenchment.

Another sign is increased brand switching. This is tolerable as long as the "right" customers switch. However, when high-value users prefer to switch, there is a serious problem. Often, switchers have stopped believing that their supplier is an appropriate long-term partner. This may be caused by an ineffective innovation strategy which can't be fixed on short notice. What can make switching even more dangerous is the bandwagon effect. Customers may consider their supplier as more risky if others switch. This is a very dangerous feedback loop.

The principle success factor of a customer lock-in strategy is the growing entrenchment of high value-customers in your customer base. This practically guarantees a stable and profitable revenue stream in the future. It protects businesses against competition and price wars. Be very much aware of what drives entrenchment of the customer base and which instruments are effective in boosting it.

SUMMARY

The value of the customer base should be managed like any other asset of a company. This is the idea of customer equity management. Its principles can be readily applied to the management of customer lock-in strategies. The consequences for monitoring the success of a strategy are fundamental. Lock-in calls for measuring the degree of brand entrenchment with customers from core markets and not only brand adoption ("counting customers").

19

Organizational Imperatives for the Customer Lock-in Strategy

Every change of strategy requires an adaptation of the organization. These changes may refer to the formal structure of an organization, the core values and beliefs of its members, the skills needed by them, and the systems and processes supporting their work. But above all, it refers to the behavior of top management with its role model function within the company and as the driving force of organizational change.

ORGANIZATIONAL BELIEFS: THINKING IN TERMS OF CUSTOMER LOCK-IN

Thinking in terms of customer lock-in runs somewhat contradictory to the popular customer satisfaction doctrine in which customer satisfaction is regarded as synonymous with profits. Lock-in is something that many customers don't want. It can be a source of severe customer dissatisfaction. The customer lock-in strategy may require a change in thinking of the members of your organization. The first step in achieving that is to explain the rationale behind the customer lock-in strategy.

One reason why customer satisfaction is such a popular strategy is because it puts the customer into every employee's focus. This is good, but it does not mean that customer satisfaction is the ultimate goal. The relationship between satisfaction, customer lock-in and profits needs to be explained.

A central idea of part 1 is that customer lock-in moderates the relationship between CS and profits. With strong lock-in, this relationship can break down. In parts 2 and 3, we looked at lock-in strategies and instruments and found that customer lock-in greatly enhances the ability to:

1. bind high-value customers on the basis of brand-specific investment, and
2. extract additional profit by selling value-enhancing complements and upgrades that allow customers to leverage their brand-specific investment.

With that approach, a win-win situation is created. The customers win because they will receive a sufficient return on their brand-specific investment. Companies win, because they stabilize and increase their revenue stream and shield it from competition. The reasons for higher profits are the increased probability to sell add-ons and upgrades with switching costs at profitable prices.

The possible misunderstanding lies in thinking that customer satisfaction loses its importance altogether. This is dead wrong for two reasons. First, if the customer base is exploited by simply milking customer switching costs through temporal price discrimination, the company reputation will suffer. This will severely restrain the ability to attract new customers and eventually cause excessive switching—strategy doomed from the beginning. Second, the win-win situation outlined above implies satisfied customers, not dissatisfied ones. Customers will only engage in brand-specific investment if that investment produces an appropriate return. This return comes from being able to profitably use brand-specific knowledge, the bonus points resulting from brand-loyalty, or leveraging the investment into a proprietary technology by adding valuable complements. A strategy aimed at customer lock-in must deliver that to be successful. Then there is little reason for customer dissatisfaction.

To understand this, it helps to look at the whole situation from the customers view. From their perspective, engaging in brand-specific investment is precarious. Don't necessarily make it less precarious but make sure that it has a happy ending. This raises the issue of who is responsible for generating "happy endings." Who is in charge of making sure that customers receive a proper return on their brand-specific investment? The answer is everybody. It requires an effective R&D function that focuses on innovations that provide sufficient value to justify brand-specific investment. Engineers and marketers together should coordinate new product development in order to find optimal combinations of benefits, insurance, and switching costs for different customer segments in the market. The sales function must have the ability to identify high-value prospects, build relationships to them, and monitor the level of brand entrenchment. It must provide feedback to the other functions concerning the success of the strategy. The implementation of a customer lock-in strategy cannot be delegated to a single function in your organization.

To coordinate this effort is a top management task. If management already feels task-saturated, they must rethink their priorities. With customer lock-in, we are talking about securing and enhancing the ultimate source of business profits; in other words, revenues. What can be more important than that in our volatile times?

ORGANIZATIONAL STRUCTURE

Organizational structure is built upon two pillars: the differentiation of tasks into functions and divisions including the allocation of decision-making authority, and the coordination of people and functions to achieve organizational goals. Superior organizational design allows for more efficient coordination of value creation processes and, at the same time, enhances the company's value creation skills, leading to competitive advantage.

For a successful customer lock-in strategy, the organizational structure should reflect the need to coordinate operations, R&D, marketing and the sales and service function for different customer segments in a market. This can be done in different ways.

- Choose the classic functional approach (purchasing, operations, R&D, marketing, etc.) in which the coordination of segment-specific strategies is the responsibility of top management.
- Differentiate by products that appeal to different market segments. This is a good approach if these divisions are dissimilar in the approach to R&D, operations and marketing. One option is to differentiate along customer segments which prefer distinctive combinations of value and switching costs. Here is an example. Division A markets a no-frills product with little or no switching costs; B, a high quality/medium switching costs package; and Division C, a high end/high switching cost bundle.
- Differentiate by acquisition and retention tasks, creating divisions that focus on the needs of new and old customers. This model is suggested in the customer equity management literature. A top manager for each division is solely in charge of all acquisition or retention efforts, and coordinates the functions to that effect.

- Simultaneously differentiate by function and customer segments, creating a matrix organization.

Which approach of differentiation works best depends on which interfaces are created by differentiation and how important they are. For most companies, it makes sense to differentiate along functions because this generates the well-known benefits from functional specialization. After all, to manage R&D well is very different from the management of operations or sales. At the same time, closely coordinate the acquisition and retention of customers as they get locked-in. If the focus is on few or only one segment of the market (for example, customers who prefer the high end/high switching cost package), it's probably true that it's better to integrate acquisition and retention and differentiate by functions.

The situation looks different when a product portfolio begins to diversify and different bundles are marketed to different segments of customers. The more dissimilar these segments are, the more efficient it is to create separate divisions catering to these segments. Figure 19-1 depicts the matrix solution, in which functional specialization is accompanied by this type of segmental differentiation.

Don't overestimate the power of organizational structure to coordinate differentiated tasks. The invisible network of relationships between employees can be just as powerful. The core beliefs within your company are also powerful motivators—or roadblocks.

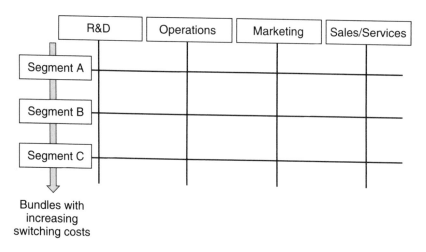

Figure 19-1: Organizational Implementation of the Matrix Structure

A MARKETING IMPERATIVE: BALANCING ACQUISITION AND RETENTION

One of the great problems in marketing is handling the interaction between acquisition and retention programs. Think of the AOL case. The equity of an installed base can be severely damaged by up-front discounts to seemingly "new customers." What needs to be done is coordination of acquisition and retention programs to achieve a balance between the goal of enlarging the customer base and profiting from lock-in of entrenched users. Effective coordination requires the following.

1. To assess the impact of various acquisition strategies (special pricing or special product bundles to first-time buyers) on existing customers' propensity to end or sustain their relationship with a product or company.
2. To design and implement strategies that take interaction into account and are capable of improving customer equity.

In the case of AOL, it's necessary to know how many existing AOL customers can and wish to end their contract when exposed to introductory offers targeted at first-time buyers. It is safe to assume that this proportion increases with the height of the up-front discount, the extent of its availability, and the shorter contracts with customers are. This enables one to choose that up-front discount that generates the maximum increase in total customer equity. Some old customers can be tolerated to quit and come back as "first-timers" because acquisition instruments cannot be designed that do not interfere at all with retention programs. A different approach is to find a way to keep the segments separate. In the AOL example, this would imply up-front discounts not being available to old customers, or designing an incentive that does not appeal to them.

Balancing acquisition and retention is not easy but is crucial and should be recognized as a key function within an organization.

20

An Outlook
on Lock-in Strategy

The longest journey begins with a single step. Going for customer lock-in raises a number of interesting challenges. Deliberately engage customers in long-term relationships by creating switching costs. The profit potential of such relationships is obvious. It is also obvious that rational customers will change their purchasing behavior and the way they select suppliers.

This last section of this book is dedicated to the changes in the marketplace which affect the customer lock-in strategy. Some are particularly relevant:

- The emergence of networks which serve a market in an integrated system of suppliers
- The rise in customer power
- The diffusion of the internet economy
- One-to-one marketing

BUILDING NETWORKS: TEAM UP TO SPEED UP!

A single product strategy offers limited potential for customer lock-in. This is where risk for customers is the greatest. There is little potential to leverage brand-specific investment. A portfolio of products and services on the basis of the same idiosyncratic technology presents less risk for several reasons. It allows customers to leverage their brand-specific investment and for a step-by-step engagement in switching costs. Customers can stop at any stage that is optimal for them. An extensive portfolio also signals the suppliers' commitment to the market because of the sunk costs involved spent on R&D and marketing. As such, it is a signal that this supplier is "here to stay." The fact that it is costly makes it credible.

Developing this possibly extensive portfolio requires the deployment of resources a company might not have. Many companies sometimes team up to speed up. They build networks in "which a cluster of actors collaborates to deliver the highest value to the end consumer and where each actor is responsible for the success or failure of the network."[1] Look for potential network partners up- and downstream that share a similar vision of a market in which customers are locked-in. What are the benefits to generate for which customer segments? Which technologies should be employed? What are the resource deficits of your company in implementing that vision? On that basis, develop an idea of how the optimal portfolio looks and who the best partners to contribute to it would be. Candidates show a strong fit with the value-creating capabilities needed which you cannot develop in a timely fashion. But they must we willing to be allies, depending on what you can bring to the table. Figure 20-1 summarizes this approach.

A word of caution: alliances have been touted as a remedy for many ailments, but rarely do they deliver. Each alliance member has its own goals and intentions. Be aware of this simple fact. Think of what your goals are and pursue them rigorously. Staying at the center of a customer lock-in strategy means that partners help in developing brand-specific switching costs by providing add-ons or complements for various market segments, but the core of the future business stays with you. Alternatively, you can decide to become a peripheral player in a network dominated by other partners. Both are viable options. Which option to choose depends on whether your resources are critical to the success of the network. If they are, stay at the center. In each case, direct access to customers is critical to build a brand and gain insight into their preferences.

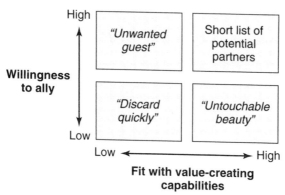

Figure 20-1: Finding Partners for Alliances

---

1 Source: G. Bitran, P.F. Bassetti and G.M. Romano (2003): Supply Chains and Value Networks: The Factors Driving Change and their Implications to Competition in the Industrial Sector, Research brief, Center for eBusiness MIT Sloan School of Management, Number 3. Available at: http://ebusiness.mit.edu/research/Bitran_SupplyChain.pdf.

RISE IN CUSTOMER POWER

Customer lock-in neutralizes the rise in customer power we have experienced over the last 20 years. Increasing customer power has been disastrous for many companies' profits. Three sources fuel the trend towards increasing customer power:[2]

- The increasing number of choices and alternative brands
- Cheaper access to information for customers
- Customers' control over information about themselves

Essentially, more competition increases customers' power. More customer power drives prices and profits down. Switching costs reduce customer power. Lock-in makes the supplier a temporary monopolist. This does not mean that there is no competition in markets with switching costs. As we can see in the game console industry (an industry with significant switching costs), this competition can be fierce. It means that after customers have chosen their brand, their flexibility to turn to alternative sources of supply is limited by the height of the switching costs. Customers still have a lot of power in markets with switching costs, but only if they haven't made a brand choice yet. In the ERP software industry, many customers are effectively locked-in because they have made substantial brand-specific investments. Differentiate between new buyers and entrenched users in a market segmentation. There is a huge differential in power between them.

With switching costs, degrees of freedom are added to your strategy. In the perfect market—what economists call the "friction free economy"—you are reduced to being a price-taker. You sell at market price or not at all. The very essence of competitive strategy is to avoid this situation. Achieve a competitive advantage that allows premium prices to be charged or a superior cost position to be attained. Customer lock-in can greatly assist in achieving that goal.

INTERNET ECONOMY

The rise of the internet economy raises a number of issues that are worth discussing in the context of customer lock-in. One of the most interesting hypotheses about the internet is that it reduces customer switching costs, because information can be collected faster and cheaper for internet-savvy users. More infor-

---

2 Source: http://www.tompeters.com/your_world/2003_08_01_ppr_archive.asp.

mation makes customers more powerful as they compare more alternative offerings at low information search costs. This, of course, is true. The internet presents a wealth of information and can be used to that purpose. The website www.travelocity.com has a superior ability to perform complex price and quality comparisons between airlines in a few seconds.

Switching costs are not primarily about information costs (the cost of collecting purchase-relevant data before brand choice), but about the brand-specific investments buyers are required to perform after they have made their brand choice. Switching costs are about brand-specific learning, bonuses for accumulated purchases, or technological lock-in. This is a different story and it has little to do with the internet economy.

The danger of the internet economy concerns the declining price level in markets for information goods as the result of declining information costs. Information goods are goods which present no uncertainty or risk after the purchase has been made. All their qualities can be evaluated before picking a brand. In such markets, the more customers know, the lower price levels are. Products and services with switching costs are not information goods. They are experience goods. It takes some time for the consumer's brand-specific investment to produce the intended return. It takes a long-term relationship to the supplier to generate it. Experience is needed to find out whether the right brand choice has been made. The internet economy can't help here.

The internet can play a significant role in the exchange of experience among users. The Cisco bug bulletin is a good example. The pooling of information allows new buyers to make a more conscious brand choice. In a manner of speaking, the internet can accelerate the reputation building process.

ONE-TO-ONE MARKETING

"One-to-one marketing" is one of those dreadful buzzwords that should have died a long time ago. It describes a scenario in which marketers can go at acquisition and retention targets with a "razor-sharp"[3] approach, designing and timing offerings in a highly individualized fashion. Don't be fooled. One-to-one marketing is and has been daily business in many industries such as

---

3 Source: Blattberg, R.C., G. Getz and J.S. Thomas (2001): Customer Equity: Building and Managing Relationships as Valuable Assets, Harvard Business School Press, p. 195.

the capital investment industry. Just ask sales engineers at GE how they sell power plants. The answer has always been the same: after intensive and time-consuming negotiations with the customer and to her detailed and highly individual specifications. The result—no surprise here—is a highly individualized bundle of hardware and service that is very unlikely to be repeated.

One-to-one marketing is sold as a new concept in consumer industries in which companies offer a limited number of product varieties to anonymous markets. Their principal acquisition instrument is the use of mass media. But don't think that Procter & Gamble and the likes are seriously thinking about developing disposable diapers to one kid's individual specifications (weight, diet, and so on). In B2C, one-to-one basically means that companies design their communication with consumers in a more individualized way. In reality, little will change as a direct result of that communication. One-to-one marketing is simply an issue because new communication tools (internet, email, and so on) are much more cost efficient and customizable than older alternatives. It costs BMW little to nothing to send an email to, say, 1,500 preselected 5-series owners in Germany of whom they know that they like to ski and have just bought their new BMW offering a certified roof rack and ski box. One-to-one marketing can do its share to increase brand preference and/or initiate some additional cross-selling. The little problem that needs to be solved is collecting, storing, and updating a lot of customer data on purchases, demographics, and preferences, and to be able to perform it. BMW says this system costs millions and the payback is still to be seen.

Customer lock-in through brand-specific investment is a much more powerful tool to increase brand loyalty and stimulate cross-selling. The BMW owner receiving this email can accept the offer or go elsewhere. There are so many aftermarket brands around, he will probably get a better deal if he shops around. But if BMW's roof rack system would be proprietary, he has no choice but to buy at the BMW dealer as he is technologically locked-in. With BMW, the complements business would be theirs. A rather more appealing outlook, don't you think?

BIBLIOGRAPHY

Abrahamson/Fombrun 1994, available at:
http://www.comp.nus.edu.sg/~tlee/books_jie2.pdf

Aldershof, T.L., and F.T. Schut: Switching Behavior of Consumers on Dutch Social Health Insurance, Proceedings of the 4th European Conference on Health Economics, 2002.

Arthur, B.: *Competing Technologies, Increasing Returns, and Lock-in by Historical Small Events,* in: Increasing Returns and Path Dependence in the Economy, edited by B. Arthur, University of Michigan Press, 2000, 13–32.

Arthur, B.: Increasing Returns and Path Dependency in the Economy, The University of Michigan Press, 2000.

Barnes, J.G.: Close to the Customer: But Is it Really a Relationship?, *Journal of Marketing,* 10, 1994, 561–570.

Berry, L.L.: Relationship Marketing and Service Perspectives from 1983 and 2002, *Journal of Relationship Marketing,* vol. 1, 2002, 59–77.

Bitran, G., P.F. Bassetti and G.M. Romano (2003): Supply Chains and Value Networks: The Factors Driving Change and their Implications to Competition in the Industrial Sector, Research brief, Center for eBusiness MIT Sloan School of Management, Number 3. Available at: http://ebusiness.mit.edu/research/Bitran_SupplyChain.pdf

Blattberg, R.C., G. Getz and J.S. Thomas (2001): Customer Equity: Building and Managing Relationships as Valuable Assets, Harvard Business School Press.

Borenstein, S.: Selling Costs and Switching Costs. Explaining Retail Gasoline Margins, *Rand Journal of Economics,* vol. 22, 1991, 354–369.

Burnham, T.A., J.K. Fels and V. Mahajan: The Antecedents and Consequences of Consumer Switching Costs, Journal of the Academz of Marketing Science, 2003, 31, 109–126.

Carson, S.J., T. M. Devinney, G.R. Dowling and G. John: Understanding Institutional Designs within Marketing Value Systems, Journal of Marketing, 63, special issue 1999, 115–130.

Cole, H.L. and Kehoe, P.J. (1996): Reputation Spillover across Relationships: Reviving Reputation Models of Debt, NBER Working Paper 5486.

Farrell, J., and P. Klemperer: Coordination and Lock-In: Competition with Switching Costs and Network Effects, available at www.nuff.ox.ac.uk/users/klemperer/lockinwebversion.pdf, 2001.

Fay, C.J.: Royalties from Loyalties, *Journal of Business Strategy*, vol. 15, 1994, 47–50.

Fombrun, C. and Shanley, M. 1990: What's in a Name: Reputation Building and Corporate Strategy, *Academy of Management Journal*, Vol. 33 Issue 2, 233–258.

Hallowell, R.: The Relationships of Customer Satisfaction, Customer Loyalty, and Profitability: An Empirical Study, *International Journal of Service Industry Management*, vol. 7, 1996, 27–42.

Heide, J. B., and A. Weiss: Vendor Consideration and Switching Behavior for Buyers in High-Technology Markets, *Journal of Marketing*, vol. 59, 1995, 30–43.

Herbig, P., Milewicz, J., Golden, J. (1994): A Model of Reputation Building and Destruction, *Journal of Business Research*, vol. 31, 23–31.

Hess, M., J.E. Ricart: Managing Customer Switching Costs: A Framework for Competing in the Network Environment, University of Nevarra Working Paper, 472, 2002.

Houser, D., and J. Wooders: *Reputation in Auctions: Theory and Evidence from eBay*, Working Paper, Department of Economics, University of Arizona, October 2001, source: http://bpaosf. bpa.arizona.edu/~jwooders/revision.pdf.

Kim, M., D. Klinger, and B. Vale: Estimating Switching Costs: The Case of Banking, *Journal of Financial Intermediation*, 2003, 1–23 (in press).

Klemperer, P.: Markets with Switching Costs, *The Quarterly Journal of Economics*, May 1987, 377–394.

Kreps, D. M., Wilson, R. (1982): Reputation and Imperfect Information, *Journal of Economic Theory*, vol. 27, 253–279.

Lee, J., J. Lee and L. Feick: The Impact of Switching Costs on the Customer Satisfaction-Loyalty Link: Mobile Phone Services in France, *Journal of Services Marketing*, vol. 15, 2001, 35–46.

Lee, K. and P. Lotz: *Noise and Silence in the Hearing Instrument Industry*, Working Paper, Copenhagen Business School, 1998, available at: http://www.accenture.com/xdoc/en/ideas/isc/pdf/NGES_RN7_Connecting_Enterpris_Solutions.pdf.

Lee, T.S., and I. Png: Buyer Switching Costs: On-Line vis-à-vis Conventional Retailing, Working Paper, School of Computing, National University of Singapore, July 2002.

Lohr, Steve (2003): *Hewlett Now Wants to Be Your Copier Company, Too*, New York Times (Internet Edition), November 17th.

Mandhachitara, R., P.G. Patterson and T. Smith: Switching Costs as a Moderator of Customer Satisfaction: An Example in Thailand's Service Industry, Proceedings of the ANZMAC 2000 Conference, 767–772.

Mariñoso, B.G.: Technological Incompatibility, Endogenous Switching Costs and Lock-in, *The Journal of Industrial Economics*, vol. 49, September 2001, 281–300.

Nielson, C.C.: An Empirical Examination of Switching-Cost Investments in Business-to-Business Marketing Relationships, *Journal of Business & Industrial Marketing*, vol. 11, 1996, 38–60.

Nilssen, T.: Two Kinds of Consumer Switching Costs, *Rand Journal of Economics*, vol. 23, 1992, 579–589.

Proenca, J. F., and L. M. de Castro: The Nature of Corporate Banking Relationships for Relationship Marketing, in: Proceedings of the 7th Conference on Relationship Marketing, Berlin, 2003, 251–266.

Rao, A. R., Qu, L. and Ruekert, R. (1999): Signaling Unobservable Product Quality Through a Brand Ally, *Journal of Marketing Research*, Vol. 36 Issue 2, 258–268.

Richtel, M.: The Lines are Busy as Cellphone Clients Switch, *New York Times*, 25.11.2003.

Rindova, V.P., S. Kotha (1999): Building reputation on the internet: lessons from Amazon.com and its competitors, working paper, University of Washington, available at: http://us.badm.washington.edu/kotha/personal/pdf%20fil es/amr_final.PDF

Santema, S.: Relationships in a Dyadic Perspective, Proceedings of the 7th Conference on Relationship Marketing, Berlin, 2003, 131–144.

Shapiro, C. (1982): Consumer information, product quality, and seller reputation, *Bell Journal of Economics*, Vol. 13, Issue 1, 20–35.

Shapiro, C., and H. Varian: *Information Rules*, Harvard Business School Press, Boston 1999.

Shapiro, C., and H. Varian: Switching Costs: Note to accompany *Information Rules*, available at http://www.inforules.com/ models/m-switch.pdf.

Silver, M.: The Costs and Benefits of Moving to Sun's Star Office 6.0, 7/1/2002, Research Note Number: DF-16-5396, Gartner Group (ed.), available at http://gartner2002.hec.ca/ research/107800/107883/107883.html#Bottom%20Line.

Tirole, J.: The Theory of Industrial Economics, MIT Press, 1997.

Wathne, K.H., H. Biong and J.B. Heide: Choice of Suppliers in Embedded Markets: Relationship and Marketing Program Effects, *Journal of Marketing*, 65, 2001, 54–66.

Viard, V.B.: Do Switching Costs Make Markets More or Less Competitive? The Case of 800-Number Portability, Working Paper, Graduate School of Business, Stanford University, 10/25/2001 (draft), available at http://faculty-gsb.stanford.edu/viard/personal/PDF/port.pdf.

Weigelt, K. and Camerer, C. (1988): Reputation and Corporate Strategy: A Review of Recent Theory and Applications, *Strategic Management Journal,* Vol. 9 Issue 5, 443–456.

Yoon, E., Guffey, H. and Kijewski, V. (1993): The Effects of Information and Company Reputation on Intentions to Buy a Business Service. *Journal of Business Research,* Vol. 27 Issue 3, 215–228.

INDEX

ABOUT TEXERE

TEXERE, a progressive and authoritative voice in business publishing, brings to the global business community the expertise and insights of leading thinkers. Our books educate, enlighten, and entertain, and provide an intersection where our authors and our readers share cutting edge ideas, practices, and innovative solutions. Texere seeks to cultivate, enhance, and disseminate information that illuminates the global business landscape.

www.thomson.com/learning/texere

ABOUT THE TYPEFACE

This book was set in 11/13 pt ITC New Baskerville. The Baskerville typeface was created in the 1750s by John Baskerville of England. Credited with originating the English tradition in fine printing, John Baskerville was appointed printer to Cambridge University in 1758. George Jones designed this version of Baskerville for Linotype-Hell in 1930. In 1978, Mergenthaler Linotype Company released a revised and updated version of Baskerville that included additional weights with corresponding italics. Through a licensing arrangement with Linotype, ITC released New Baskerville in 1982. This typeface, known for its delicate and graceful style, is well suited for use in longer blocks of text.